FIVE AMBER BEADS

RICHARD ARONOWITZ

ISBN 9789493418219 (ebook)

ISBN 9789493418196 (paperback)

ISBN 9789493418202 (hardcover)

Publisher: Amsterdam Publishers, The Netherlands

info@amsterdampublishers.com

Five Amber Beads is part of the series New Jewish Fiction

Copyright © Richard Aronowitz 2006

All Rights Reserved. No part of this publication may be reproduced or transmitted in any form or by any means, electronic or mechanical, including photocopy, recording or any other information storage and retrieval system, without prior permission in writing from the publisher.

Lines from 'Baby Me' by Lou Handman, Harry Harris and Archie Gottler © Copyright 1939 by ABC Music Corp., a division of Bourne Co.

'The Story of the White Cup' from *A Clear Space on a Cold Day* by Roger Mitchell (Cleveland State University Poetry Center, 1986) reproduced by kind permission

Postscript II 'Coming to German' © Richard Aronowitz 2025

All rights reserved.

Richard Aronowitz has exerted his moral rights in accordance with the Copyright, Designs and Patents Act of 1988.

*for Charlotte, my bright flame,
and for all those candles extinguished*

I am not sure why I want to tell it
since the cup was not mine and I was not there, and it may not have been white after all.
When I tell it, though, it is white, and the girl to whom it has just been given, by her mother,
is eight. She is holding a white cup against her breast, and her mother has just said goodbye, though those could not have been, exactly, the words. No one knows what her father has said, but when I tell it,
he is either helping someone very old with a bag, a worn valise held in place with a rope,
or asking a guard for a cigarette. There is, of course, no cigarette. The cattle trucks stand with their doors slid back. They are black inside, and the girl
who has just been given a cup and told to walk in a straight line and told to look like she wants a drink of water, who screamed in the truck
all the way to the station, who knew, at eight, where she was going, is holding a cup to her breast and walking away, going nowhere, for water.
She does not turn, but when she has found water, which she does, in all versions of the story, everywhere, she takes a small sip of it, and swallows.

'The Story of the White Cup' by Roger Mitchell (from *A Clear Space on a Cold Day*)

PART I

'Here in the democracy of the dead is a marvellous mosaic of a great city ...'

Harold Evans

1

He is a blank canvas. He is an unwritten page. He woke up in this room, with its simple desk, functional chairs, and four single beds, almost one year ago now. He did not know who he was or how he had got here. He was told that he was in hospital in New York, but did not recognise the name.

He looks about seventy-five years old, although he could be older. He has rheumy, bright blue eyes and a way of holding his hands together as if he is shaking them in greeting with himself. Nurse Kowalski named him Christopher when he was brought in to the hospital, after the street in SoHo near to where he was found lying on a pavement, semiconscious, with a broken nose and an egg-sized lump on his head. No one knew whether he had been mugged or hit by a car. No one had seen anything happen. He had no identification on him when he was found: all he had were the clothes he tried to stand up in and a few nickels and dimes in his pockets. He had no name and no history. The doctors here diagnosed retrograde amnesia, a condition that wipes the mind's photographic plates clean, erasing your remembered past. Time is the only possible cure.

Christopher is not slow or stupid, don't make that mistake. Despite his age, his blue eyes pick up everything that goes on around him, like a magpie gathering gems of information. Everything fascinates him, catches his attention. He is like a wrinkled, newborn baby that tastes the world for the first time. He stares intently at me, at the doctors and the nurses, focusing all his energy on not forgetting who we are. He suckles the air, fondles the furniture, the light switches and the lamps, turns the items on his food tray over and over, learning their shapes, their names. The great city beyond the windows with their white blinds is still outside his reach, beyond understanding.

Over the months since he has been here, the hospital and the police have tried to determine his path through life and time that led to his lying without memory or possessions on a street in downtown New York. The clue that they thought might be most useful, that he speaks English with a faint eastern German or Polish accent and is fluent in those languages as well as in French, has proved of little value. Articles have appeared in local and national newspapers in the States, as well as in Britain and Germany and on the Internet, but no one has come forward to claim him as their own.

The headlines have called him the MYSTERY WITH NO HISTORY and the MAN WITH NO PAST. He calls himself Christopher Street and understands the tragedy of his birthright. He has tried to help the doctors and the police; you can see him straining to look backwards into his life. He says that he just sees blankness. The doctors say it is just a matter of time.

I was in New York for my research when I stepped off the kerb without looking and a yellow cab slammed into me. I suppose that I must be absent-minded or have a death wish. I was lucky: no head injuries and only a little loss of blood. I was left lying on West 53rd Street with both legs broken, towered over by a crowd of passers-by and high-rises, in turn. The bones are still mending and I am confined to bed, unable to walk until I am released from the traction in three weeks' time. I have been in New York for six weeks now, nearly all of that time here in this blank room. I am counting the days until I can see my girlfriend Caroline and England again.

The other two beds in our room are empty, and there is little else to do but talk and write. Nurse Kowalski has persuaded the hospital administration to lend me a laptop computer; the nurses have named me 'The Writer', assuming mistakenly that I am well known at home, if not here in America. The nurses and Christopher's doctor administer food, bed baths for me, news of progress in Christopher's search for identity as he inches backwards into his life with the therapist, a surgeon of memory who shaves filigree-fine, translucent sections from the stem of human life, the tissue of human recollection. Christopher says he now remembers the smell of the *Sachertorte* that Caroline brought for me when she flew over last weekend on a visit, but does he remember it from the before or from the after?

I have become his best friend, his surrogate father, his long-lost son, his window into the world, his looking glass. Conversations with him are like travelling through a treacly, deep space. There is a slow distance between us. Christopher has no footnotes. He asks me about my life and how I got to be here in this room, hoping that my story might conjure his own back to him, might jump-start the vehicle of his life once again. As my words write themselves one letter at a time onto the virtual page, Christopher stands now and then at the head of my bed, reading over my right shoulder. Christopher's faculty for language does not seem to have been impaired by whatever accident it was that brought him here. He remembers snatches of song, passages of poetry, a few scattered names possessed by people who have receded into history, names that are meaningless to him and to the world outside. He recalls nothing at all of his own past. Yet he has perhaps as great a grasp of my mother tongue as I do, although we are both sure that his birthplace lies somewhere north of the Danube, not here in New York and not in England.

'Tcharley,' he says with the voice of a cracked bell, his tongue chiming against the rim of his white dentures, 'Tcharley, the story you have told me about the history of your family is in many ways my own. The loss of identity, a very human loss, and the reawakening.

What your story has that mine doesn't is the memories. Tell them for me.'

'I'll write what I can.'

Christopher nods like a bird and blinks once, then walks on his thin legs back to his side of the room and perches on the end of his bed, his head in his hands that are veined like dried leaves.

My name is Charley Bernstein and research is my way into life. I was in New York about a Picasso, a portrait of his lover Dora Maar called 'Tête de Femme' in the Museum of Modern Art, and about my great-uncle's diary. I am an antenna, an aerial in the art worlds of London and New York. I am a duct for information. I research Impressionist and modern paintings for three or four different dealers in each city, delving into the provenance of the works of those luminists and modernists to trace their murkier pasts; exposing their roots to see whether they might be looted art. Paintings extracted like teeth from Jewish collections during the Third Reich and sold in clandestine auctions or privately, deals done on handshakes with blood on them. I research the history of these works, but not the academic exegesis that you learn about in books. I track down where they were on any given day; find out whether their alibis are watertight. I am a spy, a snoop, a master of surveillance. At least, that is what I do as my day job. At night I write up what I find between the lines of enquiry, in the spaces of the day.

Almost every week there is a new painting to research. The money involved for the galleries that employ me is as inflated as the egos in the world in which I operate, feeling like an interloper dishing up an unpalatable eastern European rigour and imagination into a world where signet rings, double cuffs, the right dress and the right address say more about you than you could ever possibly have to say for yourself.

During moments of crisis in history, art – after human life itself – is often the quickest to devalue. It is reduced from a luxury good, a prized commodity, to a common currency. I can only guess how the Picasso, now worth many millions of pounds on the open market, might have been exchanged for three hundred Reichsmarks, buying for its starving owner a year's ration of bread. What happened to the millions who had nothing to trade, who had nothing with which to bargain except their lives?

It was of course not just German-Jewish families that were affected: as the net of nationalism spilled out across Europe, the looting of art and antiques, jewels and gold and silver, cars and houses drew out the pus, as the Nazis themselves saw it, or sucked out the lifeblood, as I prefer to see it, from thousands upon thousands of individuals and families. We are not what we possess, but when it is taken away from us our means of escape are cut off.

Why does Julius Neuberger, the owner of a small but very smart gallery in his own likeness on the Upper East Side and the dealer acting for the museum while it tries to sell the painting, worry about its history? Why does he concern himself about its provenance after it left the artist's studio? Because the descendants of the Jewish families who lost their worldly goods to the Nazis, and more often than not their lives, now want their art and antiques, their jewels and their gold and silver, their family houses back. If someone stole something from you, would you not try everything you could to find out who had taken it, to get back what was rightfully yours? The descendants know who the culprits were; finding the objects themselves is usually the difficult part. Every time an important painting or sculpture created before 1945 changes hands now on the art market, deals done on handshakes – one hopes – without blood on them this time, its history is mapped, its terrain charted, so as to be sure that the new buyer will not have a lawsuit on his hands when he finds that the masterpiece rightfully belongs to a surviving heir of some family from Brussels or Hamburg, Arles or Vienna, or a person living a quiet life in some country far away from Europe.

I researched the Dora Maar before I came to New York from my third-floor office room in London on Conduit Street, above a furrier that attracts daily protests from the anti-fur lobby, shouting with collective Tourette's. She was painted in Picasso's studio in Paris and sold through the dealer Ambroise Vollard there to a collector in Munich, shortly before that visionary promoter of Impressionist and modern art died in 1939. She was quickly sold again, to another German with the name Rosenberg who lived in Berlin, and later put for auction at an Austrian auction house in June 1942. This would normally set every alarm bell ringing, as a painting consigned by a collector with a Jewish name to a wartime auction in Austria usually implies forced liquidation of stock at best and liquidation of life at worst. I happen to know, however, that Rosenberg was in this case Horst Rosenberg, an Aryan with a Jewish surname. He probably sold the painting to finance his lifestyle; his legendary love of cars and women, his delight in entertaining (it is even said that he once held a banquet for the Führer at his *Schloss* just outside Augsburg). The portrait was bought at the auction by a Swiss collector not attending the sale in person and whose son, Maximilian Lüning, emigrated with the painting to New York in 1952. It was from him that the Museum of Modern Art acquired it privately. The painting would then seem to be in the clear, this time.

Caroline is a lecturer in Byzantine art history in Cambridge and I shuttle between the hearth of home and The Smoke where money crackles like green fire. Caroline's research into Byzantine art explores the labyrinths of mind and imagination of the ancient world; my history is altogether more recent, and much more personal. I was also in New York to donate my great-uncle's diary to the Sczazy Institute, having transcribed his seismic handwriting, translated it from the German and taken down all the evidence I need. These days, I find myself thinking less and less about my paid investigations and the artists who poured their lives onto canvas, and more and more about my world, or rather the lives of the people that brought me into it.

It is almost four in the morning when I hear a movement in the room and open my eyes to the night. The moonlight coming through the slats of the Venetian blinds stripes the sides of the beds nearest the windows and the legs of the tables and the chairs. Christopher is kneeling at the foot of his bed, whispering words that come to me only as fragments from distant childhood. '*Vater unser, der Du bist im Himmel ... Unser täglich Brot gib uns Heute, Und vergieb uns unsere Schuld, Wie wir vergeben unseren Schuldigern ...*' He is reciting the Lord's Prayer: 'Our Father, which art in Heaven ... Give us this day our daily bread, And forgive us our trespasses, As we forgive them that trespass against us ...'

Meeting Christopher has got me thinking about how fragile the threads that hold our memories together are, those fine silk filaments that string our life's sentence along. This is my deposition of the facts before it is too late for memories.

2

Succinum

Amber is freighted with the weight of time and history. The tears of trees, turned from emotion to an almost-stone over tens of millions of years. It has more of the fluvial than the alluvial about it; a slow river of sap that holds life and memory, inert yet intact inside itself like a kernel or an essence. While fossils in stone are shrouded in the inner space of a cold, hard womb, those in amber shine out through reds, oranges or yellows as if caught in a permanent, beneficent X-ray.

Five amber beads, ranging in size from a dessert grape to a ripe plum, and the colour of old blood. On my mother's death, they were passed down to me in a rich blue, velvet pouch with a black cord drawstring. They had come down to my mother from her mother, in turn; dark-eyed Miriam who had died, before my mother had reached her fourteenth birthday, in Treblinka. My mother's beads, whilst holding no inclusions in their warm depths, contain an abundance of life beneath their satin sheen and static shine. Sixty-five years on, I can only imagine how my mother's mother wore the necklace of beads. How many were there on their fragile thread before it broke and an uncountable some were scattered on the beads' journey into my hands? How did the sunshine, filtering through the blinds in her apartment, burnish them? How did my mother hold them on her journey to England, spilling like bright points of fire from her hands as she arrived on that morning, alone aged eight and speaking not one word of English? A new home and a new language away from the ones she already knew. Harwich is a place perhaps more accustomed to departure than arrival; a place for blustery goodbyes on cold quaysides and fish-and-chip dinners before tearful embarkation; of ferries for the coast of Holland and northern Germany. Harwich was my mother's port of entry into her new life, after an overnight journey by boat from Holland swept by the waves of sleep, darkness and loss. No lullabies that night from her mother. The amber beads were a warmth in her pocket. A set of silver knives, forks and spoons cradled in her knapsack like a kind of currency; her mother had been left them in turn by another family, with the surname initial H, before their deportation to the camps. I eat with that cutlery to this day, tasting the sharp shock of metal every time I bite too hard into these memories that are not my own.

On 26th July 1939, the day on which my mother arrived in England, the Glenn Miller Orchestra recorded 'Baby Me' with Kay Starr, written by Archie Gottler, Harry Harris and Lou Handman. It goes:

> Baby me, come on and pet me, honey, baby me
> You know you get me when you give me that affectionate talk
> Like 'darling, dearie, precious, pretty',
> I could even go for 'itty bitty'...
> Baby me, because I love it when you baby me
> The beauty of it is that I love you and you love me too
> So Baby, won't you baby me

An Emergency Imposition of Duties was passed on the import of woollen cloth into the Republic of Ireland, stating:

> A duty of customs at the rate of an amount equal to forty-five per cent of the value of the article shall be charged, levied, and paid on every of the following articles imported on or

after the 26th day of July, 1939, that is to say, woven tissues (other than floor coverings) made wholly or partly of wool or worsted which (a) are imported in the piece, and (b) either (i) are not less than fifty inches in width, or (ii) are less than fifty inches in width and have no selvedge or have not more than one selvedge, and (c) are less than seven ounces, but not less than five and one-half ounces, in weight per square yard, and (d) are of a value of not less than one shilling and sixpence per square yard, and (e) are not otherwise chargeable with duty.

My mother's import was burdened with another kind of duty, a duty of remembrance for her family; the leverage of separation imposed by the history taking place around her. Selvedge: the edge of cloth so woven that it cannot be unravelled, or a border of different material or finish along an edge of cloth intended to be torn off or hidden.

Across the world in Austria, a Franz Schütter, the son of a porter, born in Linz on 30th May 1920, was issued with a *Wehrpass*, second type, on the 26th July 1939 by the *Wehrbezirkskommando* Linz, part of *Wehrkreis XVII*, service number *Linz z. d. D. 20/1/54/9*. It might have been him who shot my grandmother with a single bullet to the head or switched on the engine that pumped the diesel into the gas chamber. Or it might have been him who saved the lives of one hundred and twenty-seven Jews, mostly women and children, near Kraków in August 1940 in an unrecorded act of heroism and humanity, before walking unnoticed into history.

To mineralogists amber is *succinite*, deriving from the Latin *succinum*. I give you a happenstance, scattershot account of one day in that long hot summer before war. A biopsy drawn from the flesh of history: succinct abridgement of my mother's arrival from Germany. I know no more than the facts.

Bernstein

It is often said that roots anchor you, but they can also set you adrift. My mother lost her religion to the English boarding school that welcomed her as a refugee into the bosom of its Christian teaching. She lost her accent and received a new set of vowels and vocabulary, attitudes and beliefs. The Christmas tree supplanted the Hannukah candles, and her mother had already lost the daughter that she knew by the time my mother heard of her own loss in a letter from the Red Cross in 1944. And yet her dark eyes deep as wells and her refusal to deny herself the right to speak out, loudly and without shame; her refusal to bow to the tight-lipped path through life of her adopted country always gave the game away, made people aware that she was from elsewhere and that she hid another history behind her. Most people just didn't know where that elsewhere was.

My mother married out and I was christened, just like my three brothers before me. Growing up, we didn't know what questions to ask. My mother's history was as remote as the dark side of the moon. What child can understand his roots, the seeds from which he springs, when his parent's need is to conceal, to store away beyond retrieval? I grew up playing in streams, kicking puffballs, unearthing molehills, as curious as any other boy around my way. Only later did I realise that the bright moon did have a darker side; only later did I learn that a whole parallel what-might-have-been mirrored what was; that Jewishness ran in my family alongside my father's gentle Englishness, an otherness to counterbalance the languor of home.

Does identity have its own complex set of imperfect fractions? My mother was not, in fact, fully Jewish although she paid fully for it. Her father was a German of part-Jewish background who had a short affair with her mother, Miriam. He had originally been the husband of Ida, Miriam's sister, but she died while still in her twenties and he took up with Miriam instead. My maternal grandfather left for America in 1930, shortly before my mother was born, and was never heard of again.

Apart from Ida and Miriam, there were my other great-aunt, Hedwig, and my great-uncles Albert (who had fled to Melbourne, via Holland, by the outbreak of World War Two) and Isy. Their parents, Lajzer Pinkus Bernstein and Perla Fajga Wermund, married in 1897 and moved from Łódz in what is now Poland and what was then White Russia to Wuppertal-Elberfeld near Düsseldorf, on what has always been German soil, in 1910. My mother was born with her mother's family name, as the father she never met took his with him when he boarded the boat to the New World.

Bernstein is the German word for amber and means 'the stone that burns'. These blood-red beads burn a hole in the pocket of my mind and my story spills out from their surface. I took on my mother's name when she died of stomach cancer at the beginning of the 1990s, a life of containment – she sometimes said in her last months – manifesting itself in a disease that led her to bring up the truth with increasingly desperate and frequent regularity. I took my mother's family name to keep her memory alive, and to remember all those candles extinguished.

Elektron

The most common amber in western Europe comes from the countries surrounding the Baltic Sea, namely Poland, Russia, Germany, Denmark and Lithuania. It comes from a deposit known as the Blue Earth, which lies below the water table and extends out into the Baltic Sea. Storms can rip out amber from this bed, which dates from the Upper Eocene to the Lower Oligocene, and wash it up onto the shores. Lumps of this amber are also occasionally washed up in Britain on the East Anglian, Kent and Yorkshire coasts after a storm.

My mother's amber beads retraced this route from the Baltic to England's east coast, by way of train and sea and amidst the storm of the times, held in her small, frightened hands. Amber, when rubbed against woollen cloth, is given a charge of static electricity. The Greeks called this substance *elektron* for this remarkable property. I like to think that my mother's beads carry a small charge of their own, the electricity of history arcing across the generations from that to this, from extinction to renewal, loss to memory. So we have it for another time between soup and potatoes, as great-uncle Isy used to say.

3

Iconologists spend their days researching likenesses; they know faces, understand physiognomy. Their field of expertise as scholars is Greek and Russian Orthodox icons. 'Icon' derives from the Greek *eikon*, meaning image. The art that survives from the Byzantine era, from the Balkans and from Greece and Asia Minor, is mostly religious art: this is because secular art was not closeted away; it was buried under the rubble of civilisations, under the upheavals of time. Sacred images were stored away in churches and cathedrals: they were held sacred and survived in relative abundance. The likenesses on icons are of people no one has ever seen.

Byzantine art deals with the paradox of representing physically unknown but to believers very real figures: Christ, the Virgin Mary, the Saints. Later, post-Byzantine icons also wrestle with representations of God Himself. The Byzantine artisan circumvented the Second Commandment, which expressly forbids the making of false idols, by imbuing the subject of worship on the icon with the actuality of the being he represents: portrayed and portrait collide, they are interchangeable. God is in the image and is the image. Byzantine art is what Byzantine beholders made it: that is always the get-out clause for the artist. Likeness is never actual; it is the viewer who makes the association, completes the loop, trips the trip-wire, gets caught in the snare.

In the one creased black-and-white photograph I have of my mother and her mother in Wuppertal, they are standing in their sparse apartment at 37 Lothringerstrasse. The apartment is the one from which my mother heard the brownshirts goose-stepping down the street outside as a little girl. My mother must be about four in the photograph. She has curly hair and clear eyes, which would be mid-brown and hazel green if they were in colour. She has a sweet white smile that would stay the same if it could.

Standing beside them are my great-grandparents, Lajzer and Perla. Lajzer was the foreman of a weaving factory and once served in one of the numerous Russian-Turkish wars as a Russian soldier, riding during the campaign for twenty-four days and nights on the back of a camel in Arabia. How such things are possible I do not know. The fifth inhabitant of the photograph is Isy. I only met great-uncle Isy once, in 1979, when he came on a visit from Australia. Until then, my only knowledge of my mother's surviving aunt and uncles, cousins and second-cousins there was through the large white bundles that they sent every year: parcels with rainbow jumpers, old Kodak cameras, green-and-red striped belts with S-buckles, kindly thought cast-offs for their less advantaged family back home in Europe.

Isy had a heavy German accent, despite his thirty or more years in Melbourne, and white hair tonsured by time. I remember three things that struck me as odd about him: he pronounced the town Reading like the activity, rather than the proper name. He would grab my bowl of porridge on those winter mornings if I did not clean it out, scraping the bowl down to the glaze. And he had numbers tattooed on his left wrist. I had never seen anyone with tattoos close-to before. I did not know anything else about him, did not understand how he related to my being here in our family's stone cottage or how his destiny had decided my own. If I had known, I still would not have understood the meaning of gratitude at the age of nine or the human cost of that for which I should be thankful. A child asserts its right on the world to be here without the defining parameters of past or present. A child simply *is*: this is its stamp of totalitarian authority on the blank face of its new world.

One thing above all else saved my mother's life, I learnt much later. Isy was the only one of his generation of my family to be born in Germany, in Wuppertal during 1913. His four brothers and sisters were all born in Łódz, coming to Germany as children where they grew up as the only Jewish family in their long street, in a house with four floors and two families on each floor. The house was wall-to-wall with a Lutheran school, which all five children attended, sent there by a father who became disillusioned with what he saw as the German Jews' rote beliefs. He knew the Torah by heart and believed every word he spoke, sacred or profane, reciting liturgy or cursing God and man. What he did not believe was that German Jews meant what they prayed or understood the traditions that they practised.

Lajzer's children did not take part in the religious lessons at their new school. Isy was the one who perhaps took most from the education, not having had the childhood grounding of Jewish belief in the White Russian *shtetl* from which the other members of his family had come. He gravitated as a young man towards an esoteric educational and religious movement based on the principles of Christianity and went to live in Switzerland. He remained close to his sister Miriam and to my mother; and as the black light of National Socialism shone down on the Jews of Germany, as the Party's finger pointed down with its sharpened steel nail to each individual as in some perverse national lottery, he went back to Germany to try to save the lives of his sister and his niece.

His contacts in England enabled him to get my mother out on the *Kindertransport* by train from Wuppertal and then by boat from Holland to Harwich. She was a child of eight and got an exit visa, I know no more than the facts. Her mother fell foul of the authorities, of the statistics of her age and the blood of her birth and was sent to her death. Such was National Socialism's genius and such was its love.

I have always looked upon Isy as some kind of icon. Caroline sometimes tells me how much I look like him. I have a photograph of Isy taken on his arrival in Melbourne in 1947, wearing a striped suit and tie. I sometimes hold it up to the light in its heavy wooden frame: the glass reflects back my strong nose, my high forehead, my dark eyebrows and angular cheekbones, but the deep eyes that look out of the photograph are his alone. I share perhaps one-eighth of his blood, and none of his experience of the world, and do not understand how two people across the generations can look so alike. Perhaps it is just a trick of the light. Likeness is never actual; it is the viewer who makes the association, completes the loop, trips the trip-wire, gets caught in the snare.

4

It has taken me two weeks to write what you have just read and my legs have almost healed, the bones stretched and coaxed and nourished back into place. Christopher is no nearer to mending his break with the past, to penetrating the silence of his memory. Since I saw him praying that night (it seemed to me that he was asking God for forgiveness for letting his past escape him), I cannot get the image out of my mind – engraved in stark black and white – of him kneeling like a benighted hermit in the moonlight at the foot of his bed. It keeps coming back to me, etched onto my mind's plates like some copy after an Old Master painting.

Christopher does not know that I overheard him reciting the Lord's Prayer; those words and my reception of them distorted by unfamiliarity and the mute space between us. He has taken lately to strumming the Venetian blinds, to lifting them and squinting out into the world that they conceal and reveal in their reality striptease. If you are, like Christopher, confronted by a past that is unknown to you, how are you supposed to recognise it as your own? Christopher has no loved ones, no nearest-and-dearest to act as signposts on his journey back to himself. He might not recognise his former self if he stumbled into him on the street. He only knows the weight of who he is now, since his rebirth on a New York kerbside.

'Tcharley, I am so lonely here,' he says. 'It seems that no one outside knows me. I do not know myself.' He chases cold vegetables around his plate with his fork, sips his beaker of orangeade.

'I am lonely too,' I try to comfort him. 'Caroline is at home in England on her own and I am stuck here with my legs hoisted in the air, relieving myself into a bedpan.'

'Yes, but at least you have something to shit for.'

'You mean, to *give a shit* for?'

'Yes,' he says.

When Nurse Kowalski comes in at eight in the evening, she bends over to tuck Christopher's sheet in where a corner has worked itself loose. He stares inquisitively down the front of her uniform as she bends to tend to him, like a child looking for succour from the warmth of his mother. She catches the gleam in his eyes as he looks.

'Christopher, get your thievin' eyes off ma chest,' she teases him with raucous amusement.

Christopher seems lulled by the current of gentle humour swirling around him, and smiles a shy, fragile smile like a pigeon.

'Nurse Kowalski, I think I am in any case a little old for you. I do not know how old,' he says.

'They say you're as young as the woman you squeeze,' she replies, then turns to me. 'And you, Charley, you be *good* to Caroline, she's a great lady. Don't go chasin' no nurses now.'

'I don't think there's much chance of that. Your bed baths are all I get in the way of flirtation.'

We are on the fourteenth floor, which would be the thirteenth but for the superstitions of the Americans who always jump that number. Their elevators go one, two, three, four, five, six, seven, eight, nine, ten, eleven, twelve, fourteen, and up and up, tricking us into believing that nothing bad could happen here. Yet we all know instinctively, and by the smell of disinfectant and the hushed movement of surgical rigs, that bad things have *already* happened to the people ending up in the public wards and the private rooms of this hospital.

The view from our room must be spectacular in this early spring light. If Christopher does not remember what a city looks like, there is no better place to start learning. I can imagine the attenuated perspectives of the avenues from our south-facing windows, the threads of car lights strung along them like jewels at night, the skyscrapers layered into the distance one against the other like a Chinese mountain landscape painted on silk.

When I arrived in New York, it was mid-February and there was still snow on the ground, shrouding the city in a layer of innocence. I walked across Central Park to the Museum of Modern Art on West 53rd, breathing in deep gulps of the frozen air and exhaling them in great clouds of vapour that billowed up towards the sky. The trees that take in the dirty air of the city and breathe it out pure again like gills sprouting from the earth were coated in snow and the lake at the north end of the park was frozen over. It was as if the city had been abandoned and left to itself; I walked along the pathways that meander from east to west like an explorer in the wilderness between two vast continents. The jagged stone teeth of the high-rises reared up to the south of the park and along its sides, closing in on this vision of freedom.

Before my visit to the museum, I had been discussing Dora Maar with Julius at his gallery. 'She was a tortured lady, Charley,' he had said. 'These people of eastern European extraction!' he joked, winking at me in conspiratorial kinship. His parents were both Jewish immigrants to New York from St Petersburg in the 1930s. His *extraction* got me thinking about those photographs of the piles of teeth and gold fillings taken at the liberation of the camps. In the museum, Dora Maar looked back at me as if to say, 'What did you expect?'

Christopher's sessions with his therapist take place twice a week in the Roosevelt psychiatric wing on the ground floor of the hospital and he insists on walking down to them, rather than taking the elevator. I did not consider the possibility that he came back up by the same route, until the first time when I saw him emerge into our room, breathing heavily like a free diver coming up for air, his face a strident red against the silver-white of his hair. At first I mistook the exertions of motion for emotion, until I realised that what I saw was the exhaustion of the climb on his face. I think he labours up the stairs out of fear, but not of falling: he builds a mask of exhaustion to cover the profound devastation that emerges when his mask melts away.

I cannot seem to help forgetting that Christopher does not know who he is. He has lived for three-quarters of the twentieth century, if his face with its crow's-feet, its frown- and laughter-lines, his hair bleached by time and his veined hands can be read as clues. I am just beginning to open my eyes; he has seen. He has seen, but cannot remember, like a man who dreams and forgets that he has dreamt. He does not recall the Second World War, although he surely lived through it and must have been a subject or a subjugator during the Third Reich. I have tried to tell him what I know of the history of his times, but what he seems to want to know most of all is 'Tcharley, who were on the side of good; who were on the side of bad?' He is like a child who has watched too many Westerns.

There is a television in the nurses' staff room next to ours, and he spends more and more time in there, flicking through the channels. He absorbs information from the beams like a luminous watch, radiating facts and figures, soap stars and chat-show hosts when he comes back into our room. He has become a connoisseur of the trivial; I think that he understands the importance of my researches into my past, my provenance, but cannot yet see the perspectives. He has a foreshortened view of history, lasting just nine months since he awoke from who he was. I have my great-uncle's diary propped up on my chest, looking at it and my notes as I write. Great-uncle Isy began his second diary, *Tagebuch II*, when he was twenty-seven, three days after leaving his parents' hometown of Łódz, which the Germans renamed Litzmannstadt between 1939 and 1945 and to whose ghetto – the longest-existing in Poland – he had been deported in 1939 after saving my mother's life. The diary was written in a camp at Sternberg and he smuggled it out of Sternberg somehow before being deported to Auschwitz and Buchenwald. It is bound in tan-coloured cardboard that has browned and blackened through handling and age, and the spine is a fine, black cotton cloth. *Tagebuch II – Isy Bernstein* is written in the scrollwork on the front cover in faded blue ink. I have spent many days since the diary came into my hands on my mother's death wondering how it survived the journey. I have often asked myself how Isy – jumping the Death March column with a young and frightened Nazi guard and his friend, Fishel Rotstein, as the Nazis marched their ghosts from Buchenwald further back into German territory; fleeing first to Holland and then in 1947 to his brother's family in Melbourne – had managed to get the diary out of the camps. Such a survival could be punishable by death.

I did not get to take the diary to the Sczazy Institute, as I was on my way there from the museum when the accident happened. I think that I will keep it with me now. It was destined for the institute's small shelf of hand-written volumes from the camps, tools for historians of human misery. Isy's words create an almost perverse scene-setting; the facts and events he describes lull the reader into an easy familiarity with the everyday until the realisation of where he is cuts you.

5

Friday, 13th December 1940

We left the Łódz ghetto by train, punctually at ten o'clock in the morning, on 10th December 1940. It was the first time that I had been outside the barbed-wire fence that surrounds the part of the town that forms our ghetto since 26th August 1939. I am not sure why I have volunteered to leave for a labour camp. Perhaps it is because our Jewish leader, Rumkowski, promised that those who elect to go to the camps will have a better chance of survival than those who stay behind, and because I am still only twenty-seven and feel that I am fit enough to endure whatever fate throws at me.

I think of my sister Miriam and of little Eva and how they are every day. Eva is in England now and Miriam, if not already in a ghetto or a camp, is surely in the greatest danger back home in Wuppertal.

I would first like to explain how we were transported out of the ghetto. The Jewish authorities told us that we had to go to the Baluter Ring at six o'clock in the morning on 10th December and we took showers in groups of thirty men, during which all of our clothing and other items were disinfected. Even after this, I found at least four or five lice on my newly washed cap, some of which were still alive. Next we had to submit ourselves to a second examination by the German doctors that took place quite quickly and was only superficial. In the late afternoon I was searched out by a Jewish policeman who gave me a quarter of bonbons and a handkerchief with my name on it from Frau G. as a farewell gesture.

On the way we were then given thirty grams of bread and a piece of sausage. We were each given a pullover, two pairs of socks, one pair of gloves and an ear warmer – all made by Volga Germans – from the authorities. It gradually got cooler and we waited until the Third Commando of the German police took control of our transport of four hundred and fifty people. The leader and organiser, an SS Wehrmacht officer, gave short commands, and this is how we got underway.

We arrived in Poznan at six o'clock in the morning; at ten o'clock we reached our destination: Sternberg in Neumark, some forty kilometres from Frankfurt an der Oder in the old Reich.

The barrack camp to which we have been brought is still being built. It is brand new and simply furnished. The food leaves a lot to be desired in the first few days. The next meal was on Wednesday evening at five o'clock: some pea soup. Thursday morning a cup of black, unsweetened coffee and soup at three o'clock in the afternoon.

We are going to work on the Reich's autobahn. At the moment, the majority of our two hundred and fifty-strong group are sleeping on bare boards. Straw sacks and two woollen blankets have been only partially distributed. The camp authorities are civilians and their workers are Volga Germans and Czechs. Four thousand more men are on their way from the ghetto, to be distributed to similar camps. The sleeping rooms consist of two barracks, each with four rooms for thirty men. The main barracks consists of a large canteen, a latrine and washrooms. It is a new experience for us and good for our spirits that we are given unlimited potato rations to peel here for our midday meal.

Saturday, 14th December 1940

Today a commission came to inspect us. The leader of our building spoke to everyone in a friendly way and everyone is pleased. 'He is a good man,' *everyone says. We are almost no longer used to being treated like human beings.*

Monday, 16th December 1940

Yesterday I was elected block leader. Our appearance is generally a little blackened because we need to burn wood in the camp to keep warm.

I wrote to Miriam today: I pray that the authorities will allow my letter through. I simply wrote that I was alive and as well as could be in the circumstances; and that I miss her. She is my sister closest in age and temperament to me. With Ida dead from her sudden illness and Hedwig deported God knows where, Miriam is all I have left to hold on to. I was forgetting little Eva, of course. I must pray for news of her as well.

Yesterday there was margarine and Limburg cheese for our bread. The main topic of conversation today is the food. The same subjects are discussed again and again. At the moment, most people are bored and want to get to work, in the hope that they will be given larger rations when they are working.

Wednesday, 18th December 1940

Yesterday, because of our hunger, all of the block leaders came together and I was nominated to speak to the Kommandant to get our rations increased. We should be given potato soup, which is just as simple to prepare, instead of coffee in the evenings and this would go some way towards keeping our hunger in check. We went in a delegation of three and presented our proposal to him. He promised to look into it.

For the moment, we are not yet working and nothing will happen before the holidays. It is more than fifteen degrees below freezing. It is interesting that today already more than half of the workers want to go back to the ghetto: this is all because of how little to eat there is. Yesterday evening there was five hundred grams of bread with a slice of sausage. This hunk of bread, which is less than half a small loaf, must last each of us for three days. One still cannot buy anything, only postcards and cigarettes. We have twenty briquettes to burn for every twenty-four hours. We must burn them at night, because with our two blankets we could otherwise freeze to death.

Thursday, 19th December 1940

Today we behaved a little like animals when the food was distributed. The camp authorities and the guards team could hardly hold us back, we pressed so hard around a small amount of extra soup that was being distributed. Shortly afterwards the Kommandant came in with a written order, which I had to read out to the barracks' team of workers. The words I had to read out were as follows: 'We are not allowed to leave the barbed-wire enclosure around us without permission. Furthermore, half a loaf of bread must last us for at least two days. Resistance to this and refusal to follow this order will be punished by two days without food and possible handing over to the police. The Kommandant decides the penalty.'

Today we went to work on the railway in a group of twenty men. In this frosty weather it was a beautiful walk and we were able to make ourselves at least a little warmer through the work. At twelve o'clock we were back and were given, according to the marks we have learnt to make on our bowls, a little more soup at midday. Walking through a little town I saw the windows decorated for Christmas; everything was very quiet, as if it had died. Only now and then a woman brought her cakes to be baked at the bakery.

Sunday, 22nd December 1940

Yesterday we went back to the railway station in a group of thirty men; we had to unload a wagon of work material, such as rails, under the direction of the current leader and foreman of the unit. I was allowed to write up the entries in his logbook. This work was good for me and for the others. I have to keep note of the team that must at present go to work at the railway station, as well as the amount of hours they work.

In the afternoon when we were back at base I was suddenly called to see the Kommandant by one of the men from the team of German guards. It was proposed to me that I might like to take on the role of Unterführer. I would have liked to continue working with the leader of the unit who is sympathetic to me, but the elders of the nine blocks want to give me this role, which I have accepted. Our camp consists of a work force of two hundred and forty-six. My duties are to represent the interests of the work force to the Kommandant. I also have to announce the day's food provisions to be prepared, and am responsible for the kitchen itself, that is to supervise the cooking pots themselves so that the cooks do not steal meat or other delicacies. This position and this form of activity is what the whole team of workers whom I must look after would like to do.

By today, the post had still not been sent off. I am now experiencing a time in which I will learn how difficult it is to want to be fair to everyone.

Wednesday, 25th December 1940

Even today, nothing to feel of the holiday. It is seven o'clock in the morning and I am standing in the kitchen and supervising, as it were, the breaking of the bread. Yesterday evening I lay in bed and thought of my loved ones back home. It has now been three Christmases that I have spent in such a way so far from the spirit.

Yesterday, Christmas Eve, there was great uproar. The dealing in cigarettes was brought to light. We were all loudly called into the yard. Four men were being beaten. No one admitted to dealing in the cigarettes. The Kommandant ordered that the whole block would get no food until those who were responsible admitted what they had done – which he eventually retracted.

We received bread three times this week. We are still starving. Many want to go back to Łódz again. There are two very ill people amongst us, one of whom has some sort of pulmonary illness and no doctor. There is no water to wash with, because each day all available water is brought to me on a cart for the kitchen. Because of this, lice are establishing themselves and we have no repellents against them. All this, with the little nourishment for us, creates a starved moroseness in the men.

Saturday, 28th December 1940

Yesterday I went along to the railway. We were stacking wood. Each of the two hundred and fifty men wants to come along and I am only able to choose thirty to forty for this. There is often anger and bad feeling. Furthermore, it is also difficult to listen to each man's wishes with equanimity. Then I heard from the Kommandant that the post is now going off and everyone is very pleased about this. Also from today I will have a special room with the Clerk. I am particularly happy about this, as I hope now and then to be able to be alone for an hour or so.

I have been ordered by the Kommandant to draft the camp's laws, which is a task made all the more difficult by the fact that I am writing my own sentence.

General Orders:
1. The barrack camp is surrounded by a barbed-wire fence.
2. This is to be regarded as the boundary of the camp and is not to be left without special permission.
3. Wake-up call begins punctually at 5 in the morning.
4. Breakfast lasts from 5.45 until 6 in the canteen.
5. The block elders are responsible to the Unterführer for the punctual march to work.
6. The time of the march to work is decided by the camp's Kommandant and will be announced at the given time.
7. The block elders are jointly responsible to the camp's Kommandant and the Unterführer for a full personnel count upon the march to and the return from the place of work. In special cases such as sickness, accident, etc., the block elder must make his report to the Unterführer.

8. The midday meal will be served after the work period, also in the canteen and in order of room.

9. At nine o'clock in the evening lights must be turned out and each person must be punctually in bed by this time.

10. While the lights are on, the rooms are to be blacked out. The room elder is responsible for this.

11. The Unterführer is chosen by the camp's Kommandant. He is responsible for the entire organisation of the camp's inmates and is directly responsible to the Kommandant.

12. All commands of the Unterführer are to be followed immediately.

13. The Kommandant has the sole right to administer punishment. The Unterführer is responsible for carrying this out.

14. It is brought to your special attention that the Unterführer gives his commands in my name.

15. Whosoever goes against these orders, or behaves contrary to them, will be punished.

THE KOMMANDANT

6

It is almost time for me to be pushed out of the womb of this room, to emerge from the ash-grey birth canal of the corridors and the mother ship of the hospital. I am wheeled on a rig to the X-ray room, for one final check before the pins are pulled, the bolts unbolted and the circular saws set in.

One week after the traction and the casts are removed, my legs are still as spindle-thin as Christopher's. I see their flesh beneath my hospital gown for the first time in more than two months. They look pale and etiolated, like bamboo. The bones have knitted together beautifully, the doctors say, but I had not countenanced the atrophying of the flesh, the muscles wasting without use. I had not considered that I would not be up as soon as the casts were off. It is some days before I can stand even with the aid of crutches.

The geographical route out of New York is one that I have travelled many times before. The psychological terrain is an unfamiliar one: how to say goodbye to Christopher, to leave him like an orphan to his fate.

'Tcharley, send my love to Caroline. Tell her, next time I see her it will be in England, even if I have to stow away on an aeroplane.'

'At your age, I should hope that your visit to us will be a *little* more dignified,' I reply.

Christopher winks and smiles at me like a child preparing for some practical joke. Despite the lightness of the exchange, it is not difficult to read the impending return to loneliness in his eyes. I cannot help wondering how Christopher will cope once his pattern is disrupted again, when I am no longer a feature on his daily landscape.

'Do you believe that I will find out who I am?' he asks.

'Yes, I do,' I say, but the words come with difficulty and I try to smile, to reassure him. Christopher also knows that the time that has now passed since his past loped away like a shadow means it is unlikely he will ever catch up with that *doppelgänger* again.

I hug him as if I have not held another human being in my whole life.

'Christopher, it has been an honour to meet you; an accidental honour. I would be very happy if you could visit us in England.'

'The police have said that I cannot travel without a passport, and that I cannot get a passport until they know my name and place and date of birth,' he replies.

'I will help you all I can,' I say, adding, '*Warte nur, balde ruhest du auch*' – that line from Goethe which says *Just wait; soon you too will find peace*. I hope that he understands, and his look of sadness and gratitude says that he does.

Christopher and Nurse Kowalski walk with me to the hospital entrance to hail a cab. The traffic streaks by on York Avenue, and the passers-by form a steady stream of humanity, grown from the insignificant ants they appeared to be from the Fourteenth Floor.

Nurse Kowalski, by way of a goodbye, says, 'Live a little, Charley, and send us a postcard from home.' I think that it will take me a while to learn how to live the way I used to. The cab takes me up over the great span of the Triboro Bridge, across the East River, and snaking through the back streets of Queens, past the light industrial units and the hard sell, the shop-fronts with their grilles pulled down like shuttered eyes, and out to the Rockaways and JFK.

The flight makes an incision over the frontal lobes of Canada and

Greenland, an operation viewed on the monitor embedded in the seat in front of me, then slices out above a sea of wilderness. I sleep like the dead during the Atlantic crossing, or as if I have been anaesthetised. Between places and between lives.

I cantilever myself on the crutches through the 'Nothing to Declare' customs lane at Heathrow, thinking about how much I have brought back with me from New York. The customs officials do not move, but give me a cursory glance on account of my stubble and stuttering progress.

'Charley!' Caroline's beaming face emerges from behind a crowd of unsmiling drivers holding placards with peoples' names, casting the nets of their glances wide around the arrivals hall to catch the big fish they are to drive to Central London, Berkhamsted or Tring.

My trajectory has taken me, in the space of a half-day, from one embrace to another, and this one is home.

As Caroline drives me back to Cambridge, we begin where we left off at the end of her visit to New York. She tells me about her research, about the Byzantine intrigues of academic life at Cambridge. Who is thinking what and who is seeing whom.

'Charley, the scrubbed corridors of the Manhasset Hospital are no preparation for the mean streets of Cambridge: these ivory towers hide all sorts of dirt,' she says.

As we drive down those streets, through the labyrinth of the one-way system to the heart of the city, it begins to rain and I realise that it is the first time I have seen rain since I left England more than three months ago. It pummels the pavements, sends litter scurrying into culverts and drains, chases pedestrians into doorways. Our house seems to have changed, to have shrunk into itself somehow, as if it is built on quicksand.

It has become almost a ritual for me to take out my grandmother's beads when I return from time away, holding them in my hands and gathering in their warmth. The beads anchor my thoughts. They gleam with a lustre that cannot be muted; a deep red anger that cannot be abated.

7

New Year's Eve 1940–41

I am sitting in my little room and the old year is just coming to an end, while the new one is beginning. Today I am looking uncertainly back on my decision to come here, and I think that it was – contrary to my other work comrades – the right decision. My long-held desire to have a quiet room with a few hours for myself alone in the day has finally been brought to fruition. I share a small room with the Kommandant's clerk. There is a double bed and a stove, which is moved into a second room every morning and brought back each evening. Two carpenters have made a little cupboard and a little chair. I also got a table today.

Yesterday I found a counterfeit food card which I gave in and, on the command of one of the men from the team of guards, had to show it to the Kommandant. Everyone was called out to the yard while we went individually through the rooms looking for the faker. I had to ask throughout, but no one came forward. Everyone had been called to the yard but still no one came forward, and we were told that we would have to walk around the yard until someone did. When someone admitted it, he was beaten by an inmate.

The midday meal distribution always costs me some health. We already have a large and worrying amount of sick people in the camp, without medical help or any medication. I am tormented very often at each visit to my room, and asked how it looks to me for the sick people; whether a few important medicines have been bought.

Friday, 3rd January 1941

I slept through the change from one year to the next. I am usually very tired from all the discussion and the running around in the evening, and my eyes generally shut in this very warm little room.

I wrote up the camp orders in fair copy during the course of the day and gave them to the Kommandant to read through. He read, agreed and signed them without making a change. It is the first time that I have written such orders and I am surprised that they were accepted so readily.

I decided yesterday that I am not giving out second servings at the midday meal to those who work particularly hard. From now on I am having slightly less distributed at first, so that I can make a second serving later, which everyone is happy about. Today I had the second round distributed two hours later, and everyone was also pleased about this. We did not need to use restraint once. The Kommandant was also in agreement with this.

For two days a cold northeast wind has been blowing here. Day and night the snow is driven into mounds in certain places. Everything ices over, even the pots in the kitchen. It cannot be ruled out that in this situation we will have a lot of sick people and I cannot see any salvation for us unless we can hope for a little luck in our fate. One man's shoulders and armpits are full of sores, and he moans in pain day and night. Another has had his pubic hair cut off because he had rubbed the area with petroleum against lice and this had led to a dangerous skin inflammation. We have no means of defence against such things; no medical help. I am constantly called for and asked for advice. Toothache and fever are also common – and I cannot help them. There is also a man with pulmonary illness amongst us and he is not well. The Kommandant came in to see me and to speak about this and I proposed the idea to him of establishing a special room for the sick in the third barrack block, which is still empty. He agreed to this plan and I will carry it out tomorrow. Generally, the camp authorities are not bothered whether people are ill or not.

Sunday, 5th January 1941

Forty Reichsmarks has arrived from Miriam, along with different letters from home. How my heart leapt with the news that Miriam is still alive! Miriam and I must have thought of each other on the very same day, and we must each have sat down to write to one another in an act of loving solidarity across the five hundred miles that divide us. She is in danger in Wuppertal, with her only daughter taken away from her by fate; I am held in captivity here, not knowing what my future will bring. God rest the souls of Elajzer and Perla who are no longer alive to witness these terrible events.

This evening during my daily rounds everyone made protests to me about the food situation. Every day the same thing and still I can be of little help. Today, while I was writing in the Clerk's room and the Kommandant came back from his morning inspection round, he said – outside the inmates were doing exercises to keep warm – 'You, what is the Unterführer doing sitting here while the men are outside doing their exercises? Go out – the people are more keen when they see their Unterführer' – which I did.

The block elders got together and begged me to write a letter to Rumkowski on behalf of the 246 camp inmates. This is intended as a complaint concerning the lack of medications and a doctor and Rumkowski's broken promise to us concerning the payments our families were to receive if we volunteered to come here.

To the Eldest of the Jews, Herr Rumkowski, Litzmannstadt ghetto:

I would like to bring the following to your attention: I, the undersigned, have been appointed by the Kommandant as the camp's Unterführer, after the person you proposed indicated that he could not be considered for this post. The situation in our camp is such that, because of the weather, we still have not been able to go to work and we have earned nothing. We refer to the transport cards printed by you in which it is clearly stated that our families will receive a weekly twelve Reichsmarks to ease their living situation. You can imagine both how surprised and angry we are here to learn from our loved ones back home that you have not kept to that official promise. According to the transport cards, our families were to get the first 12 Reichsmarks on Wednesday 11th December; on the 18th December the second payment; on 25th December, the third and already by now the fourth. We have heard from home that you have restricted these payments to the first one, so that we had to accept loud and clear that our wives, children and parents there should continue to starve and freeze, as we have not gone to work. We further find ourselves in the situation that we are completely without medical help. The weather conditions and other circumstances in no way allow this. We heard from the Kommandant that, according to the official decree, in addition to workers and kitchen personnel, a doctor and helpers were also meant to belong to the transport.

There can be no other explanation than that you consciously overlooked this, and thus brought us into increased danger for our lives. At the moment there are twenty seriously ill men amongst us, and we have no idea what to do with them. All the same, the camp authorities have told us that you have to provide all medication and medical assistance. In these things we are completely lacking. You will see from all this that we are in this regard not in an enviable situation. You will also understand that if we Jews cannot help each other, the German authorities will have less interest in doing so themselves.

We therefore turn to you with the fervent pleas of our families to spare them from these undeserved hardships, and to provide us with a doctor and medications as quickly as possible.

Yours sincerely, Isy Bernstein

THE UNTERFÜHRER

8

One bright early morning in June, a month after returning from New York, sunlight slants through the windows of my train bound from Cambridge to King's Cross. I am looking at the shadow the train casts as it moves over the flat fen landscape, the extended crenellation of each coach and the notches of light between them. The silhouette of the train could be any train; it is a generic shadow that my train casts. It could be a goods wagon: we are stuffed in like cattle. The generic transports us towards genocide: it could have been me. When I kissed Caroline goodbye this morning, her forehead warm under her tousle of blonde hair, it might have been the last time I would see her.

Dora Maar was one of a long list of Picasso's conquests: the little man was a great painter and just as great a womaniser. When he met Dora, a Yugoslav-French beauty who was also blessed with a piercing intelligence, he was married and already had a mistress on the side. Dora was another prop to his talent, another colour for his palette, another gird to his loins. He used to see her from every possible angle, paint her in every possible facet. In 1937, at the height of his Synthetic Cubist period, Picasso painted the 'Tête de Femme' showing her with a vivid, acid-green face and mournful purple eyes framed by thick black hair tied back in a cornflower-blue bow. Picasso's trick in love was to be in three places at once; to keep his wife, his mistress and his girlfriend all blissfully fulfilled and blissfully unaware of the complex web of infidelities into which they were spun like bright and exotic insects. Picasso's trick in his Cubist paintings was to see things from several different perspectives at once: to create in the viewer the effect of walking around the three-dimensional subject whilst standing still in front of the painting. Dora's face is side on to us in profile, but we can see both of her eyes, both of her nostrils, both of her ears. She sees, smells, hears the world around her with the immediacy of a living thing. But she is only a figment, only oil on canvas. She is the dark side of the moon brought round to the front. Such was Picasso's genius, such was his love.

Caroline is my muse, my Dora, although I am no artist and any rendering of her would result in a clumsy, unintentional Cubism all of my own. I am more faithful to her than Picasso ever would have been. Dora was dark and her spirit was dark. Caroline is blonde and has a spirit filled with light, a light that has enough darkness woven into its fabric to give it weight. There is no syllogistic relationship between the outward appearance of things and how they are, there is no axiom or equation that states that what rewards the eye will also reward the heart. But it happens to be true with Caroline. She has a good soul: you can see it in her cornflower-blue eyes and in her smile that blinds you.

It is not an easy trick, holding different facets of a personality in your mind's eye at the same time. History always seems to take place in a linear narrative, in straightforward black-and-white. In the hierarchy of hatred of the Nazi race laws, bloodline always came above belief. Isy could not simply opt out of their plan for his race. Who was Isy? An interim answer must be: a man, a Jew and a Christian. The same could be said of me.

When Isy died of an asthma attack in 1989 at the age of seventy-seven, he was cremated after a civil ceremony in a modern brick crematorium in Melbourne. Tattoos are a sacrilege of the flesh in the Jewish religion; the fire that consumed his body – another taboo, as Jews believe that the dead must be buried, not burned – swallowed the numbers on his left forearm. Isy's great-nephew Mark whispered the *Kaddish*, the prayer for the dead, beneath his breath as the coffin slid towards the fire.

What might a man do to survive? No, what might a man do to make himself able to live with himself? Just as raking light over a painting throws up reliefs and contours of pigment and areas of reworking that you cannot see in direct light, so extreme situations adumbrate the stature of a man. It was a common tactic to have a Jew elected as the vice-leader of a camp, as the human megaphone held to the mouth of the inhuman machine. *It is brought to your special attention that the* Unterführer *gives his commands in my name.* What does he need to survive? He needs food, water and the nourishment of mental stimulation, of human contact. Isy writes his diary in a camp whose inmates are permitted to receive and send letters and postcards, leading everyone to believe that everything is going to be all right, that no one will get hurt. I would like to construct a model of history in which the countless millions of letters sent to addressees who have moved house or who have been forcibly removed from their homes reached their intended recipients, instead of piling up unread in the communal hallways of apartment blocks. I wonder, if all those messages had got through, what history would look like then.

9

The exchange of letters is a commute between distant stations. Christopher sends me commuted sentences, lines of incarceration, words out of a snow-blind silence. Caroline has taken to calling him 'Our Man in New York', as if he is a news correspondent or social commentator, but Christopher has no news, no Stop Press from his past.

The Manhasset Hospital New York, 12th June

Hallo Charley,

I guess you are home now. Life here is not the same. How is Caroline? Still no news about me. I am very much looking forward to coming to England and to seeing you both one more time. Write soon.

Love, Christopher

P.S. Nurse Kowalski says 'Hallo' too.

Going back to London and the room that I call my office is charting a territory with which I feel unfamiliar, one that I am unable to traverse. It is not that the stairs to the third floor are the problem: my legs are strong again and I take the steps two at a time. It is the reason for being here that I find so foreign to me now. Julius has sold the Dora Maar to a private French collector, and the painting has been repatriated to its country of birth, to be swallowed up in the cold embrace of some bank vault or the overheated atmosphere of a mock-Gothic chateau in the south. She had become a friend to me, and I feel a strange sense of loss.

I am waiting for a new painting whose past needs to be exorcised or absolved. High summer in the art world is a quiet place to be. The anti-fur protesters on the pavement below my window, outside the door of a boutique specialising in the pelts of mink, ermine, badger, rabbit and fox, punctuate the silence with their cries of mock rage. Otherwise, the streets are wrapped in the shroud of a dry and windless heat, and the telephone is dead.

I am like one of those men who, having been fired from their place of work, still go on with the pretence that they have something worthwhile to do with their day. They leave their homes and their wives, with their faces shaved and their briefcases full of guilty subterfuge, to sit in a local library or a park. I wonder how many Jews across Europe during the Third Reich hid the truth from their families in this way when they were sacked from their positions as professors, doctors, lawyers, clerks, waiters and waitresses. I still have the place of work, its rent counting down the half-life of my small savings, but have no paid research during my first few weeks back. I have decided to devote myself again to my history, and to helping Christopher find his.

The Internet is a tool as vital to my research as a bugged telephone or a telephoto lens is to a private eye. Tap any name into a search engine on the Internet and more often than not, if you know where and how to look, you are soon walking down the digital pathway to its owner's front door. My mother, Eva Bernstein, does not emerge from the blankness when I search for clues to her arrival in England, however. She seems to have vanished into the eternal silence of unrecorded history. The famous dead make constant, ghostly appearances and the living fill page after page of the results of my searches with their *Welcome to my Webpage!* self-affirmations. The search engine's magical algebra conjures up a galaxy of pages that might make any nuance of a connection with the parameters of my request, but none is an exact match with the DNA of a mother who was more than simply flesh and blood to me. She was where I came from.

I have found an organisation through the Internet that will help me perhaps to uncover some trace of my mother's arrival in England, to follow the paper trail leading back to her entry into her new life.

Dr Lilian Gottschalk
Jewish Refugee Committee
14 Conduit Street
London W1

1st July

Dear Dr Gottschalk,

My mother, Eva Bernstein (1931–1992) came over from her birthplace Wuppertal-Elberfeld in Germany on a Kinderstransport by boat from Holland to Harwich and then by train into Liverpool Street station shortly before the war, on 26th July 1939. She died seven years ago, and I remember a few years before her death she saw a trailer for a television programme (on the BBC, I believe) requesting that those children who came to England on one particular train contact the programme-makers as adults who had survived the Holocaust because of these transports. My mother said that she was on that train, but found it too hard to get in touch, and I am still wondering whether there might exist more documentary details of her arrival in England?

I would be grateful to hear from you and hope that you can help me in my research.

Yours sincerely,

Charley Bernstein

Five days after writing to Dr Gottschalk, I receive a reply from her, telling me that the London Metropolitan Archives has kept all documents relating to the *Kindertransport* children's arrival here until now; a lost property office for the children's identities. A week later my mother's *Kindertransport* card arrives at Conduit Street in an anonymous envelope marked *To be delivered by Walk Officer on Second Delivery*. My mother's card, with a black-and-white photograph of her wearing her hair in bunches that pull at my heart, is another piece of evidence, another material witness to her journey here. It was the passport to her survival; carried by the Head of the train, one for each head of human cargo.

The legend above the photograph reads: 'This document of identity is issued with the approval of His Majesty's Government in the United Kingdom to young persons to be admitted to the United Kingdom for educational purposes under the care of the Inter-Aid Committee for children.' A blue stamp on the back marks its authority: 'LEAVE TO LAND GRANTED AT HARWICH THIS DAY ON CONDITION THAT THE HOLDER DOES NOT ENTER ANY EMPLOYMENT PAID OR UNPAID WHILE IN THE UNITED KINGDOM, IMMIGRATION OFFICER HARWICH, 26 JUL 1939.'

My maternal grandmother was destined for domestic service with a family of assimilated English Jews in Somerset. The payment she was to receive was their saving of her and her daughter's lives. But Isy could not get my grandmother, Miriam, out of Germany with her daughter and my mother herself became the domestic. She was collected from Liverpool Street station by Uncle Sidney, as she came to call her foster father. I imagine my mother looking around one last time at the black hulk of the train, its funnel billowing steam up towards the great glass roofs of the station, and understanding that there was no way back. Uncle Sidney carried her small, brown leather valise, with its label *Eva Bernstein, Wuppertal-Elberfeld Lothringerstrasse*, under his arm, while my mother held the one doll she was able to take with her, which she called simply *Mutti*, meaning Mummy. He took her by Omnibus from Victoria coach station to Minehead, where my mother's life began again.

Mordechai Chaim Rumkowski was the leader of the Judenrat in the Łódz Ghetto to whom great-uncle Isy wrote with the complaint about the deteriorating health of the Jews who had, like him, chosen to leave the ghetto for the camp at Sternberg. Rumkowski gave a famous speech to the remaining population of the ghetto on 4th September 1942, holding a megaphone in one trembling hand and gesticulating to the vast crowds with the other.

'A grievous blow has struck the ghetto. They are asking us to give up the best we possess – the children and the elderly. I was unworthy of having a child of my own, so I gave the best years of my life to children. I've lived and breathed with children, I never imagined I would be forced to deliver this sacrifice to the altar with my own hands. In my old age, I must stretch out my hands and beg: brothers and sisters! Hand them over to me! Fathers and mothers: give me your children!

'I had a suspicion something was going to befall us. I anticipated "something" and was always like a watchman: on guard to prevent it. But I was unsuccessful because I did not know what was threatening us. The taking of the sick from the hospitals caught me completely by surprise. And I give you the best proof there is of this: I had my own nearest and dearest among them and I could do *nothing* for them!

'I thought that would be the end of it, that after that, they'd leave us in peace, the peace for which I long so much, for which I've always worked, which has been my goal. But something else, it turned out, was destined for us. Such is the fate of the Jews: always more suffering and always worse suffering, especially in times of war. Yesterday afternoon, they gave me the order to send more than twenty thousand Jews out of the ghetto, and if not – "We will do it!" So the question became, "Should we take it upon ourselves, do it ourselves, or leave it to others to do?" Well, we – that is, I and my closest associates – thought first not about "How many will perish?" but "How many is it possible to save?" And we reached the conclusion that, however hard it would be for us, we should take the implementation of this order into our own hands. I must perform this difficult and bloody operation – I must cut off limbs in order to save the body itself. I must take children because, if not, others may be taken as well – God forbid.

'I have no thought of consoling you today. Nor do I wish to calm you. I must lay bare your full anguish and pain. I come to you like a bandit, to take from you what you treasure most in your hearts! I have tried, using every possible means, to get the order revoked. I tried – when that proved to be impossible – to soften the order. Just yesterday, I ordered a list of children aged nine – I wanted at least to save this one age group: the nine to ten year olds. But I was not granted this concession. On only one point did I succeed: in saving the ten year olds and up. Let this be a consolation to our profound grief.

'There are, in the ghetto, many patients who can expect to live only a few days more, maybe a few weeks. I don't know if the idea is diabolical or not, but I must say it: "Give me the sick. In their place we can save the healthy."

'I know how dear the sick are to any family, and particularly to Jews. However, when cruel demands are made, one has to weigh and measure: who shall, can and may be saved? And common sense dictates that the saved must be those who *can* be saved and those who have a chance of being rescued, not those who cannot be saved in any case. 'We live in the ghetto, mind you. We live with so much restriction that we do not have enough even for the healthy, let alone for the sick. Each of us feeds the sick at the expense of our own health: we give our bread to the sick. We give them our meagre ration of sugar, our little piece of meat. And what's the result? Not enough to cure the sick, and we ourselves become ill. Of course, such sacrifices are the most beautiful and noble. But there are times when one has to choose: sacrifice the sick, who haven't the slightest chance of recovery and who also may make others ill, or rescue the healthy.

'I could not deliberate over this problem for long; I had to resolve it in favour of the healthy. In this spirit, I gave the appropriate instructions to the doctors, and they will be expected to deliver all incurable patients, so that the healthy, who want and are able to live, will be saved in their place.

'I understand you, mothers; I see your tears, all right. I also feel what you feel in your hearts, you fathers who will have to go to work in the morning after your children have been taken from you, when just yesterday you were playing with your dear little ones. All this I know and feel. Since four o'clock yesterday, when I first found out about the order, I have been utterly broken. I share your pain. I suffer because of your anguish, and I don't know how I'll survive this – where I'll find the strength to do so.

'I must tell you a secret: they requested twenty-four thousand victims, three thousand a day for eight days. I succeeded in reducing the number to twenty thousand, but only on the condition that these be children under the age of ten. Children ten and older are safe! Since the children and the aged together equals only some thirteen thousand souls, the gap will have to be filled with the sick.

'I can barely speak. I am exhausted; I only want to tell you what I am asking of you: Help me carry out this action! I am trembling. I am afraid that others, God forbid, will do it themselves.

'A broken Jew stands before you. Do not envy me. This is the most difficult of all orders I have ever had to carry out at any time. I reach out to you with my broken, trembling hands and beg: give into my hands the victims! So that we can avoid having further victims, and a population of one hundred thousand Jews can be preserved! So, they promised me: if we deliver our victims by ourselves, there will be peace!'

Here Rumkowski is interrupted by impassioned shouts and cries from the crowd about other options. Some are screaming, 'We will not let the children go alone – we will all go!' and others shout words to this effect. Rumkowski replies, shouting directly at the crowd and forgetting his megaphone for a moment: 'These are empty phrases! I don't have the strength to argue with you! If the authorities were to arrive, none of you would be shouting!

'I understand what it means to tear off a part of the body. Yesterday, I begged *on my knees*, but it did not work. From small villages with Jewish populations of seven to eight thousand, barely a thousand arrived here. So which is better? What do you want? That eighty to ninety thousand Jews remain, or God forbid, that the whole population be annihilated? You may judge as you please; my duty is to preserve the Jews who remain. I do not speak to hotheads! I speak to your reason and conscience. I have done and will continue doing everything possible to keep arms from appearing in the streets and blood from being shed. The order could not be undone; it could only be reduced. One needs the heart of a bandit to ask from you what I am asking. But put yourself in my place, think logically, and you'll reach the conclusion that I cannot proceed any other way. The part that can be saved is much larger than the part that must be given away!'

Rumkowski and his wife were deported to their deaths at Auschwitz on 30th August 1944.

10

Once, when I was a child of about eight, my three brothers and I were having our evening meal around the large oak table in the kitchen of our cottage. Paul was nineteen and John seventeen and they both looked at me but said nothing. The round table was pushed up against the back wall of the long kitchen and dining room that ran from the front of the house towards the utility room, with its stone sink and its steps to the steeply banked back garden.

'*Charley?*'

'Yes?'

'There's something we want to tell you.'

'What is it, what have I done?'

'You haven't done anything, stupid, but it's important.'

'Then *tell* me.'

'You would have had another brother – a twin – but he came out dead when you were born. Don't tell Mum we told you,' my brother George said matter-of-factly.

George was six years older than me and played drums in a band. He used to practise his drum-rolls with those silver knives that my mother had brought over with her as a child from Wuppertal, the initial H on their broad handles beginning the anonymous surname of a family whose lives had ended in the camps. He broke the blades of four out of the set of six, leaving useless stubs and handles that were only fit for melting down.

I already knew about babies and how they were made, but that lifeless foetus was as slippery and unfathomable in my mind as the boiled egg I was eating. My thoughts crumbled, fell into blankness, while my bread soldiers went marching on.

My father was away working in London; my mother was upstairs resting in their bedroom under the eaves. It was hot up in her room; I do not remember now what season it was, but I do not think that it was hot outside. The heat might have been kinetic, from me running up the two flights of stairs two steps at a time. It might have been domestic, heat from the wood-burning stove in the kitchen. I can feel it now: I think that it was *frantic*, hysterical heat.

I believed that I had killed my brother. I cried and my mother comforted me in her arms. She smelled like a haven of wool and warmth; a sheltered port in my storm in a teacup lined with the leaves of a terrible omen. I told her what George had said, and she replied: 'Yes, darling, you would have had a twin brother. We wanted to call him Julian but he was stillborn. I didn't want to upset you by telling you about him before. Let's talk about it more when you are a little older.'

'All right, Mummy,' I said to reassure her, in turn. But things were very far from that way. Things would never be the same again and my mother and I never spoke about Julian after that. Even at that age I must have sensed some of what she had been through and did not want to upset her by reminding her of another loss.

The difference between eating and being fed is not just a semantic one. One is active, one passive. The active process implies life-grabbing independence, healthy nourishment, and well-being; the passive verb, enfeeblement, infantile dependency, and an uncertain prognosis. Isy's fellow inmates were forced by history to fall into this second camp.

As an eight-year-old, I did not understand that babies were fed via the umbilicus in the womb; I believed that they ate just like I did, wolfing down food with active enthusiasm. All I knew was that I must have been greedy and eaten it all, taken what should rightfully have gone to the foetus that would have become my brother, had he been allowed by me to live. I could not believe what I had done and was plagued by the shadow of a dark twin. No one told me how babies grew inside their mothers all over the world, no one absolved me of my guilt with a simple lesson in the biology of gestation until I was about fourteen, and I never dared ask. For many years I did not talk about it to anyone again. Julian walked with me to school, kicked footballs around the uneven playing field, followed me into lessons and back home again. He sat with me at the tea table and curled up with me to sleep, as snug as a bug in a rug. As cold as a corpse in a carpet. When my mother kissed me goodnight, I imagined her lips puckering into blackness like shrivelled prunes when they touched Julian's marmoreal forehead.

I still have conversations with my twin, which usually begin in my sleep and continue into my waking life, like a fog of tiredness that takes great will to shake off. When Julian comes, he comes to me as the spitting image of myself. He always catches up with me; he is always my own age. He looks like I do if I look in a mirror, but he is in stark black and white. His eyes are jet-black and his skin is beyond pale; not a radiant, bright white but a deathly neutral one. I think of him as the negative of myself. He is every bad decision I never made; every law I never transgressed; and every other life I have never taken. I think of him as the reflection of a mountain in a lake: if I am the mountain, he is its shadow going deep beneath the surface of the water, yet as flat and reflective as a steel-grey mirror.

Conversation is not the right word for what passes between us. I can never hear what my twin is saying, however hard I try. He seems to speak in a foreign language I have not yet mastered. I have always felt that Julian is driving me towards something, to justify my being here. Or driving me towards some madness. Whilst at university I saw a psychologist to try to get to the roots of my visions, which became increasingly frightening and regular in my early twenties after the death of my mother. They took on a new life of their own. I saw these visions in glorious colour, events that had not happened or actions that I had not taken but my mind thought I had.

I would stab my umbrella spike through babies' heads in their prams, poison fellow-students' cups of tea, and throw people off bridges into the Thames. I was universal cause and effect. I would spend minutes examining the tip of my umbrella for blood in the language faculty lavatories; hours watching my friends for signs of choking or spasm in my college room; nights ringing the police stations around the city for reports of bodies being washed up on the banks of the river. Not once did an untoward outward event occur to which I could inextricably and irrefutably link myself. My head was full of tides, full of a fog lit by the waxing and waning face of Julian. I worked harder and harder at my studies, becoming fluent in German as a tool to find out about my past and the history of my mother's family, hoping that when I found some answers my past might somehow leave me alone.

Lately, Julian's whispers to me at night have become ever more distant, they seep quietly and unintelligibly through the static. He sends me nursery rhymes with no reason. In my teenage years I became obsessed with CB radios, staying up late into the night to listen to the crackling voices of truckers, policemen, firemen, and other assorted loners, freaks and weirdoes like me. I thought of them as one way to drown out Julian's voice, to hear something intelligible emerge from the silence for once, receive voices through the ether that I could at least try to understand.

Rock-a-bye baby, in the tree top
When the wind blows, the cradle will rock
When the bough breaks, the cradle will fall
And down will come baby, cradle and all.

My mother sang this lullaby to me when I was a child, and I never understood its darker resonance until now. I think my mother had always been afraid of the dark, like me.

11

Wednesday, 8th January 1941

Our sick room has sixteen people in it. The Kommandant has said to me that he is going to send them back to Litzmannstadt in the next four days.

Monday, 13th January 1941

Each day we read various newspapers. According to reports, the war seems to be setting in for a long one. Everywhere people are arming themselves madly. A new phase has begun in the Mediterranean with the combined German-Italian formations.

Tuesday, 14th January 1941

Today we have had an eventful day. There was great commotion in the camp. We were called out this morning; I had no idea why. The guards' leader and the whole team of guards were present. I asked the guards' leader, while everyone was standing there, what it was about and our Kommandant turned round and snarled at me with such force that I will be able to smell his cigar until next Christmas. Someone had escaped from our camp to Sternberg and the surrounding villages to buy bread. There were calls for information and threats to the culprits. The police were there and threatened the death penalty for any repetition of this act.

We were inspecting a room and found a pack of butter and the Kommandant suspected the kitchen workers and me of having taken it. I said that I was answerable for the actions of the kitchen people. It transpired that this pack was left over from the distribution of provisions to the blocks.

Later, I went to the station with ten men and these workers received many blows from the guards' leader. After we got back, I went to see the Kommandant and told him that I wanted to speak to him. I said the following: that I wanted to clarify my position with him a little, and that I suspected that he had something against me. He replied that he simply wanted to say that I was a little too soft in my treatment of people; that I had to get more respect from them.

Sunday, 2nd February 1941

The day before yesterday I received two parcels from home. The accompanying letter from Miriam made me happy. For a long time I have felt a correspondence between our hearts which does me a lot of good. They are busy at home and I would like to see them again one more time very much.

Yesterday I received a letter from Rumkowski in reply to the letter I wrote on 5th January, in which I called for the promise of help for those in our camp.

Herrn Isy Bernstein Sternberg/Neumark

I received your letter of 5th January 1941 and its tone alienated me.

I refer you to the fact that the payments to the people concerned take place weekly. I was obliged at the beginning to stop the payments, as the workers either gave no address or, in the most part, false addresses. I therefore had to invite the relatives of each worker to get the money through my 'Work Employment' department. This was ultimately in the interest of the workers' relatives.

I concede nothing concerning the other contents of your letter, as it is written most rudely and I refuse once and for all any further correspondence with you.

Chaim Rumkowski

Tuesday, 11th February 1941

As far as my diary is concerned, one could forget the war. According to the newspapers, the field of battle is such that England – and particularly London – has been very badly hit and, as before, air raids by the English have also penetrated into the German Reich. The battles extend to the Mediterranean, where German and Italian bombers have attacked ships and English bases. The fronts in Greece seem to have seen little change and the battles in Africa are going on as before.

It seems to be slowly becoming spring. A deadly serious, indeed decisive, spring is beginning.

Sunday, 16th February 1941

It is a strange time that I am experiencing as Unterführer. I have become bolder and through this have earned myself a little more respect. It is sad that the same men with whom I used to share a barracks now call me 'Herr Unterführer', which makes me feel a little strange. Hopefully I will resist climbing the captious steps of vanity and arrogance: I can already feel how strong the seduction of this would be.

Wednesday, 19th February 1941

This morning we buried the first victim of the Spiegelberg camp, the very first of the camps nearby. Apparently, the cause was a double lung infection. The boy had just turned twenty.

Tuesday, 4th March 1941

On 3rd March German troops marched into Bulgaria. The day before yesterday, Cologne and its environs were bombed. I heard reports that Wuppertal-Elberfeld was also hit. Last Sunday I visited a Jewish family in the town of Sternberg. They were so afraid that I suddenly realised it might be better to be in a camp than back at home.

Wednesday, 26th March 1941

Today Reichsleiter Rosenberg opened an 'Institute for Research into the Jewish Question' in Frankfurt-am-Main.
   I received a letter from home today and, after a long time, I can feel the

correspondence between our hearts again. Miriam writes that she was ill for some time, but that she is better now and is going back to work.

Thursday, 3rd April 1941

Yesterday evening I called the workers to the yard and I had to tell them that one of our comrades had simply walked away from the site where we had been working in order to go begging nearby. I had to tell them that he would be **hanged** *for disobeying the camp laws. He is the third man that we have lost in this tragic manner.*

I can feel clearly that I am falling day by day and can find no resources to fight against it. How quick and effortless the way down is and how ceaselessly hard the way up again.

In Frankfurt-am-Main, according to reports, the European Jewish problem is being solved.

12

The Internet homepage for the small town of Sternberg describes the historical persecution that took place within its walls almost four hundred and fifty years before Isy's arrival there. This story is told in the legend of the *Hostienschändung*, the 'Desecration of the Host'.

The legend describes how the Jew Eleasar stole consecrated wafers from a priest in Sternberg. The Jew Eleasar crushed and cut up these stolen wafers – history seems to have forgotten why – on the 20th July 1492 and, according to the legend, blood began to seep from them, becoming known as the 'holy blood' of Sternberg.

When Eleasar's wife tried to throw the wafers into the river as pieces of incriminating evidence, their weight became so colossal in her hands that she sank into the stone beneath her feet. This stone, confirmation of the guilt of the Jews, can still be found today by the visitor to the town, built into the wall of the Holy Blood Chapel. As a result of this desecration, pyres were erected and twenty-seven Jews were burnt to death in Sternberg in an act of Old Testament retribution. The town of Sternberg prospered after this event, for by 1500 the 'holy blood' and the consecrated wafers on exhibition there were attracting thousands of the faithful on pilgrimage. Through these early religious tourists, gold and wealth came to Sternberg, and today it is a comfortable middle-class town whose labour camp during the Third Reich is not mentioned in the official history.

Caroline and I have settled back into the regular pattern of our lives again, punctuated by the metronome of my daily commute between Cambridge and London. I call it my one-track mind, which does not yet allow me to countenance any existence for myself other than the research into looted art. Perhaps one day I will become a dealer: if you have a passion for pictures and for their history, you can believe in them enough to sell them.

Caroline is writing a research paper that she has called *Mapping the Soul: The Byzantine Image of the Self*. She worries about Christopher, and I think that this essay, to be published in a journal dedicated to writing on mediaeval history, has given her a greater understanding of the tragedy of Christopher's loss, which before she only saw abstractly, third-hand through me.

Cambridge 10th July

Dear Christopher,

Caroline and I were very happy to receive your postcard. I hope that you are not too lonely in New York now that I am home.

Caroline and I will do all we can from here: we are going to write to everyone we can who might help you get a passport and travel back to Europe to find out who you are.

How is your lawyer progressing with your case?

Are the authorities still refusing to give you a birth certificate? Can you ask the lawyer to send copies of any documents relating to your case that he can, to help with our effort here?

I will telephone you when I have more news.

Love from Caroline and me, CB

P.S. Send my regards to Nurse Kowalski too.

My days in London are spent up in this third-floor room, the central panel of the triptych of windows thrown open to allow a slight breeze to penetrate this dense heat. Both floors below me seem to have been vacated for the summer; the post is shifting slowly down the entrance hall from the front door on Conduit Street, like a glacier of white ice carrying with it the earth-browns of utility bills and the blacks of hand-delivered circulars.

I have sent a letter to the United States Ambassador in Grosvenor Square and to his Cultural Attaché, asking for their support in allowing Christopher to leave New York and come to Europe to uncover the spores and the traces on the trail to who he is. The Ambassador's office has replied that, as Christopher is not thought to be British or American, there is little cause for the Embassy to get involved. Sympathy was expressed, empathy was emitted, help was withheld.

Speaking to Christopher on the telephone requires great effort despite my deep affection for him. Christopher rewinds the digital age seventy years to Bakelite with his transatlantic delays and pauses.

'Good morning, the Manhasset Hospital, how may I help you?'

'I would like to speak to Christopher Street in Room 1404. Nurse Kowalski should be on duty up there: if you put me through to the staff room, she can fetch him.'

'Who should I say is calling?'

'Charley Bernstein. I used to be Christopher's roommate.'

'I'll put you through.'

There is a click like the lid coming off a particularly tight jar, then 'The Star-Spangled Banner' seeps glutinously out of the receiver.

'Hello, fourteenth-floor staff room.'

'I would like to speak to Nurse Kowalski. It's Charley B–'

'Charley! It's me. How are the legs?'

'They're fine. How is the patient: is there any news yet?'

'Not much I'm afraid, Charley. I think he misses you. When are you coming back to visit us?'

Before I have time to reply, I hear a loud bleep from her pager and she says simply: 'Charley, keep well. I'll go fetch Christopher.'

There is another pause, then a very tentative 'Tcharley?' in a voice like a sudden gust of wind that exhausts itself in silence.

'Christopher, I've been worried about you. How have you been since you wrote? We have been doing what we can from here, but it is slow as you know.'

'I know, Tcharley.'

'We are going to get you to England with us, however difficult it is. Then you can be here with us and start to piece your life back together. I'm sure that will do you good.'

'I am praying for the day.'

'I promise that it will be soon,' I reply. 'Is Nurse Kowalski looking after you?'

'She is kind, Tcharley.'

'Has the therapist drawn out any memories?'

'Nothing. It is as if my mind's eye has gone blind.'

'Caroline and I send you our love every day. We will see you very soon. Keep strong for us.'

'I will try, Tcharley.'

Only a few days after our conversation, the paperwork from Christopher's lawyer arrives. His deposition to the federal authorities begins: '*I, a person suffering from amnesia, in the city of New York ...*' and, with the unforgettable poetry of this phrase, Christopher's story is put forward.

All the lawyer's efforts to secure a new birth certificate for Christopher so that he can be given a passport and a new life, as it were, have been rebutted by the United States authorities. They claim that he cannot be issued with a birth certificate like every infant new to this world because he is a man who has already lived the course of many years. Christopher must have a provenance as elaborate and convoluted as the paintings I research. His life of seven decades or more has surely passed through many hands, from mother to teacher, from lover to enemy, from the embrace of passion to the clutch of hate. Christopher's past is as rich as any other life but unknown like almost no other, and the authorities state that he cannot officially exist in two separate places at the same time, governed by two sets of forms that do not match. One set in New York and the other who knows where, tearing his body and mind in two across space and across time. As the authorities cannot establish who he is, as they cannot ascertain from where and whom he has sprung, Christopher is held prisoner by the paradox that he already exists physically but not officially, as far as anyone can find. Christopher cannot now be allowed to do so until he can prove incontrovertibly who he is and that he is.

13

The abstract 'art world' is far less glamorous and exciting than many people not involved in it would believe. Its physical manifestation is often shabby and worn: the auction-house showrooms still have threadbare carpets for a country-house appeal, private galleries representing contemporary artists are often two- or three-man shows. The beauty lies in the art itself, and the excitement for the auctioneers and dealers is in the money that attaches itself to the surface of things like a gloss coat or a veneer.

If, like me, you dreamt as a child of one day being a spy or a policeman, then what I do for a living is a substitute that is often nearly as complex and always much less dangerous. People hardly ever get physically hurt in the art world (unless something falls on one of them), or at least not since 1945. Given time and research, most provenance mysteries can be solved: it is often easier to establish where a painting was on any given day in its history than a person. People are not generally exhibited or reproduced in books. From time to time in the art world you meet someone who introduces a certain *frisson* of excitement into the realm of high art: a society beauty, say, or a forger. Deborah, with her frizzy hair and her over-eager laugh, falls into the second category, and I met her again quite by chance more than two years ago in the library of the Victoria and Albert Museum. I had known her ten years earlier at the Courtauld, where she read for a Masters in Paintings Conservation while I was studying modern art history. I was researching the provenance of an early Matisse still-life and she, as she confided in me much later, was carefully inserting grainy black-and-white illustrations of the two Mondrians that she had created into the pages of a catalogue for an exhibition held at a highly respectable London gallery in the 1950s. Deborah was clever: if you can cultivate the provenance and the *milieu* for a work of art or a person, the authorities and the world at large will often not notice the physical clues to the fact that all is not what it seems to be.

What makes Deborah useful to me is that she can work on paper as well as on canvas. Deborah has never been found out and, although I have always considered myself to live almost too precisely by the book, I have a grudging professional admiration for her. She creates works of exquisite beauty. They are just not what they say they are. A fake German passport for Christopher will be no difficulty for a woman who can trick the daughter of Picasso into believing that what she has in front of her is a drawing by her father from 1942. There are white lies in the world, white spells that do good, and this is one of them.

The plaque on Deborah's door on Fournier Street in the East End says: Deborah Maclean/Conservator. On this weekday morning in late July, the pared-down lines of the Georgian street, home to several famous artists and abutting the colour and clamour of the spice district on Brick Lane, are not disturbed by passers-by.

I press the bell and hear Deborah's soft 'Hello' through the static of the intercom. I say as an announcement 'How's tricks?' This is a private joke between us: I tell her that the Latin form for a female paintings conservator would be 'conservatrix', but she refuses – like an actress who insists on calling herself an actor – to use the feminine form.

Once she has moved a pile of reference books and auction catalogues from a wooden, paint-patterned chair, Deborah invites me to sit down amidst the clutter of her studio, permeated with the cloying aroma of turpentine. From our short telephone conversation she knows why I am here, but I repeat the story of how I met Christopher after my accident; how I got to know him through the agency of chance. I tell her that his story changed something in me; that the search for identity has become the meaning of both our lives.

Deborah disappears behind her easel, with only her lower half visible beneath the horizontal ledge that holds a stretched canvas, her legs tangling visually with the easel's three splayed legs. I do not ask whether the canvas is a restoration or a forgery. She says in a disembodied voice: 'So, you want me to help you get Christopher out of New York, Charley?'

'Yes. I want you to make him a German passport, the best forgery you have ever done in your life.'

'I will need to make a visa for him as well, to insert into the passport. You know, one of those green slips the passport people staple in when you arrive? By the way, where do you want me to say he was born?'

'Wuppertal-Elberfeld.'

'What are you going to call him? The authorities might recognise the name Christopher Street from when the papers reported his case. And it isn't German.'

'I don't know what to call him yet, nor when to say he was born. I'll let you know.'

I take an envelope out of the music case that serves as a holder for my scores of notes, and hand Deborah a disk that holds a digital photograph of Christopher. The photograph was taken outside the front door of the Manhasset Hospital on a digital camera that I bought from the hospital shop. The person behind the lens was a junior doctor whom Nurse Kowalski commandeered just before I left in the taxi. Christopher is flanked by Nurse Kowalski and me and is looking straight at the camera, smiling his shy smile with his white hair scraped back from his forehead. Deborah comes out from behind the easel, walks with the disk to the desk on the far side of the room and slots it into her computer. She opens Christopher's image on screen and cuts a precise square around his head with her virtual scalpel. She saves his passport photograph on file for future manipulation, leaving Nurse Kowalski and me either side of a bright absence where Christopher used to be.

'How much will this cost?'

'Charley, let's not discuss money. This is a matter of the heart. One day you can conjure up some provenance for me.'

'I don't know if I could do that.'

'What's the difference, Charley? People; paintings: both of them can cost you dear.'

Leaving Deborah's studio, I walk west along Fournier Street to Liverpool Street station, up the stone steps that sweep the length of its vast façade and take the escalator down to the trains that wait like quivered arrows before shooting in a hundred directions towards their destinations. For a split second I see my mother as a girl, standing on the concourse beneath the Arrivals/Departures board that looms overhead between the entrance to the Underground and the gates to the overland train platforms. She has her wavy brown hair in bunches and is holding a doll protectively against her chest. I look again more closely and see that it is a girl that I do not recognise who is standing on her own; one small presence in a cavern reverberating with the noise of the crowd. Then I spot her parents, smoking, to one side by the timetable stands: she has simply strayed away from the warmth and safety of loving arms. Trains to Harwich still depart from here twice every hour.

After my conversation with Deborah, which has left me with a sense of quiet foreboding for some reason that I cannot fathom, I do not want to go back to the claustrophobia of the car horns and fumes of Mayfair. Conduit Street in the summer is a duct for tourists who flood down it like a human current from the river of bodies rippling southwards in tides on Regent Street. They eddy in smaller streams up and down the streets – Old and New Bond Street, St George Street,

Bruton Street – that branch off it where it divides at the traffic lights, encountering dams of *couture* clothes, shoes and handbags as they go. I take the slow train from Liverpool Street back to Cambridge instead, which meanders through the flat countryside of Essex and rattles and sways like an asthmatic tramp, the seats moth-eaten and worn.

14

Caroline and I are looking at a fifteenth-century illuminated manuscript depicting the 'Flight into Egypt' in the Fitzwilliam Museum in Cambridge, the University's repository of the Empire's spoils of art and antiquities; the bleached bones of cultures washed up on our shores over the centuries.

The image shows Jesus of Nazareth, held by his mother Mary, riding on a donkey. She is dressed in royal blue, while He is herring-boned with white swaddling clothes. Joseph, in red hat and rich red velvet cape over a green jerkin, guides them onwards. The saturated colours gleam in the half-light of the gallery.

'So, do you feel guilty?' Caroline asks.

'What for?'

'For making your living from graven images.'

'Do you feel guilty writing about them?'

'Yes, sometimes I do. How can you do justice to the power of an image in words? Words are just skeletons; images are their flesh.'

'Darling, words – the Law, "I do", "Has the Jury reached its verdict?" – govern the world. Images are just an embellishment; they're not binding.'

'Tell that to the Flemish artist who sacrificed months of his life to this one image. Look at the intricacy of the foliage, the life in those colours, the depth of the perspective and the power of what the illumination represents.'

'It's just a pretty picture in an obscure Book of Hours tucked away in a provincial museum, if you don't believe in what it represents,' I say to tease her.

'I neither believe nor don't believe, Charley. For me, that's not the point.'

'What about the religion behind the images you study, then?' I ask.

'Who knows. I just know that they're beautiful and important.'

'Like you, then.' I give her a kiss on the cheek, and see the white blossom of her smile.

Back at home, I take out our reference copy of the Bible while Caroline is in the bath. She is splashing water over her head and back, the droplets covering her pale skin like jewels, and I intone the words of the Second Commandment in a mock-solemn voice, trying to make her smile beneath the shampoo foam.

'Thou shalt have no gods before me. Thou shalt not make unto thee any graven image or any likeness of any thing that is in heaven above, or that is in the earth beneath, or that is in the water under the earth: Thou shalt not bow down thyself to them, nor serve them: for I, the Lord thy God, am a jealous God, visiting the iniquity of the fathers upon the children unto the third and fourth generation of them that hate me; and showing mercy unto thousands of them that love me, and keep my commandments.'

Caroline steps deftly out of the bathtub, rubbing her hair vigorously with a towel: 'Charley, God sounds like a jealous husband and an even worse father. You're not going to be like that, are you?'

Before my brother John went up to Oxford to read Zoology in the late 1970s, he spent some months working in the Negev desert in southern Israel. He lived in a research enclosure and studied the habits of a bird called the Arabian babbler, *Turdoides squamiceps*, whose habitat is mainly acacia bush country, scrubby *wadis*, desert, gardens, vineyards and reed-beds.

My mother told John before he left for the desert that Fishel Rotstein still lived in Haifa where he had emigrated after the war. Fishel was the Polish Jew who became Isy's closest ally in Auschwitz and Buchenwald, the camps to which Isy was deported after Sternberg. Fishel escaped with him on the Death March further back into German territory from Buchenwald in 1945, as the American troops of the 80th Division advanced to liberate it that April.

John, recognising the importance of Fishel in the story of the Bernstein family, tried to get in touch with him during his months in Israel. He told me when we last met, when I visited him at his faculty in Oxford where he is now Senior Lecturer in Zoology, specialising in the migratory patterns of certain western European birds, that he had never got through to Fishel, that the telephone just rang and rang.

I dial the number that John was given twenty years ago and a young woman's voice in Hebrew must be saying in its aphasic timbre, 'The number you have dialled has not been recognised.' I cannot understand Hebrew and ring Esta, a friend from university who now lives in Tel Aviv. She searches the Israel telephone directory on the Internet and finds that Fishel is still listed as living in Haifa, on the same street as her mother's closest friend.

The first time that I try to telephone Fishel, on a bleached-out morning in August from the payphone on Cambridge station, I hang up after three rings. I suddenly worry what Fishel might say; I doubt that, after all the years of no contact with my mother, father or brothers, he will know who I am.

In the soothing, monotonous thrum of the fast train and the quiet seclusion of my office, I think of how my mother and her mother lived and died, and try again. The telephone rings with its foreign tone, a more guttural, resonant one then I am used to, and an old voice answers, '*Shalom.*'

'Hello, my name is Charley Bernstein. I would like to speak to Fishel Rotstein.'

'This is he. Who is there?'

'C h a r l e y B e r n s t e i n. I am ringing from England and want to ask you about Isy Bernstein.'

'I don't understand. How are you related to Isy? He had no children; no one to pass on his name.'

'I am his great-nephew. I took the name Bernstein when my mother died, as a mark of respect for her and to remember my grandmother, Miriam.'

'Then you are one of Eva's sons?' he asks. 'I am,' I reply. 'The youngest.'

There is a pause while Fishel assimilates this news. Then he says suddenly, 'It makes me so happy that I am speaking to you. I heard about you and your brothers from Isy often before he died. During the war and after he became my closest friend on this earth.' His next words, 'You are a Jew. It is hard to be a Jew,' shock me with their directness.

'The Jewish blood in my veins is a little thin now. You know, my mother's father was a German, although I have never known his name,' I say.

'Lebrecht Rittershaus.'

'Sorry?' For a moment I think that he has slipped into another language, as he has already told me that he speaks not only Polish and English, but also German, French and, of course, Hebrew. He is eighty-seven years old and I forgive him for the confusion.

'Lebrecht Rittershaus. This is the name of your grandfather.'

'Isy knew his name and told you, but never told my mother? Why do you think he did that?'

'I am sure she knew, Charley. She did not want to add another name to your burden of history.'

We speak for almost an hour, and I tell Fishel about Isy's diary and how I have become the duct for his words written in the camps. Fishel's voice is quiet as he asks, 'How did the diary come into your hands?'

'Isy must have kept it on him through Sternberg and when he met you in Auschwitz. When you both escaped, he must have taken it with him to Holland and then Australia, giving it to my mother on one of his visits to Europe.'

'No, that cannot be so. Isy had no diary when we spent those years together in the camps. The guards would have found it. It would have meant certain death. I believe that he must have smuggled it out of Sternberg somehow, perhaps even through the mail that they were allowed to send from there in the first years. Your family's German friends in Wuppertal might have looked after it for him, which was in itself a very dangerous act, and given it to your mother when she visited them after the war.'

'Perhaps you are right. My mother did go back to Wuppertal once or twice since her childhood, to see the few friends who had tried to help save her family. It must have been then that she got the diary. I wonder if she ever read it.'

'I hope that she did not. It must be very difficult. I am sure it is hard for you to understand,' Fishel replies, then changes tack. 'After Isy and I escaped on the march, we became separated from each other after many days of walking through the terrible winter countryside. When Isy had gone, as if he had disappeared into thin air, I carried on walking and walking with the young SS guard we had met. One night I hid in a barn with him and the next morning, before dawn, I stumbled across a railway line and jumped onto a freight train that eventually passed, having no idea where it was going. After a day and a night travelling with no food or water, it stopped. I crept out from the wagon in which I had been lying when it was completely dark and found that I was near Hanover.'

'Wasn't it very dangerous there for an escaped Jew?'

'In any case, I had some civilian clothes that I had managed to find after the camp, bought with bread and cigarettes that I had saved, and at that time – with the Allies advancing from all fronts and the Germans in full retreat – they were not *so* careful in their butchery. They never knew who I was. I stole eggs and chickens from farms, bread from bombed-out parts of the city, drank water from wells and street pumps.'

'Where did Isy go?' I ask.

'You can imagine what a shock it was,' Fishel replies, 'to lose him so suddenly after the time we had spent together. The young Nazi guard who had fled with us walked with us through the land hard like iron as the Allies were tearing through to reach Berlin. We were exhausted and hungry and always worried that the Russians or Americans might stop us and make us go to a refugee camp. All we wanted to do was go home. One day, a brown American army Jeep came round the corner at high speed on a narrow road that led to a bridge over a wide river. We all ran and jumped off the stone bridge into the freezing water, to avoid being hit by the vehicle or being stopped by the soldiers. We had no papers, nothing. Isy must have been swept further down the river than us. We could not find him anywhere. I was sick with thinking that he might have drowned. When the Allied victory came with the German surrender on 8th May 1945, I made my way down to Isy's hometown of Wuppertal – have you ever been there, Charley? Later, I tried to find out what had become of him. I visited your great-grandparents' graves in the Jewish cemetery there, which was to my great surprise still mostly intact, and managed by a miracle to find one family in the town whose name I knew from him. They told me that Isy was still alive and that they had heard from him once since our escape, in late April. He was in Holland and planned to join his brother's family in Australia when he could.'

'I didn't know that Elajzer and Perla were buried in Wuppertal. I'd like to see if their graves are still there and to visit them for my mother. She was very close to her grandparents when she was a little girl. So when did you next see Isy?'

'It was not until after I had gone to Israel, I think in 1950. It was in Switzerland: I remember the reunion. Isy often came back there until his death.'

'He also visited us once or twice in England. I was too young, though, to understand much about him. I remember his voice, his white hair and his tattoo from the camps that he showed us boys. And the way he ate his food.'

'I am sure it is hard for you to understand,' Fishel says again.

'I am trying. I would very much like to bring my girlfriend and someone I met in New York, who by the way must have been born somewhere near where you were, to visit you in Haifa in the autumn.

I am planning a trip to Israel for my research and would love to meet you face to face.'

'I would also like it very much, Charley,' Fishel replies, his voice now sounding tired.

'We will be coming to Israel in late October and I will call when we arrive in Tel Aviv,' I say to let him go.

We say goodbye and I feel the weight of history pressing down on me. I leave the sweltering closeness of my room and take the early afternoon train to Cambridge, walking from the station there through the town and a long way out into the Fens, away from people and what they do to one another.

15

Sunday, 20th April 1941

In Greece, the fighting continues. The Reich's flag has been raised on Mount Olympus.

Today we buried a comrade from the Pinnow camp. He died in an accident and is the second burial in the Jewish cemetery in Sternberg.

Three days ago an important visit was announced. The General Inspector from the German Penal Buildings Authority, Professor Dr Todt, was supposed to appear. Naturally there was a huge clean up and who should fail to appear but Dr Todt.

Sunday, 4th May 1941

Today at midday I received a parcel from Miriam: a piece of birthday cake, sweets, chocolate and apples. Can my punishment get any harder than being sent a piece of her birthday cake to taste and not being able to wish her a happy birthday?

Friday, 9th May 1941

According to newspaper reports, Iraq is at war with England. In Palestine, the Arabs' revolt against the Jews is becoming fiercer.

Today the news has been spreading that Serbian prisoners are to come to our camp and other camps nearby and that we are probably going to be leaving here. I hope not to Poland.

Wednesday, 14th May 1941

According to newspaper reports, Rudolf Hess has taken off in an aeroplane, against the orders of the Reich's Chancellor Adolf Hitler, who forbade him to fly on health grounds, and he has not returned. It is thought that he has ejected with a parachute over Scotland.

This week the rules in our camp have become stricter: no one is allowed out to work without wearing a yellow Star of David and we have to be accompanied by a guard at all times.

Sunday, 25th May 1941

German troops have taken the western part of the island of Crete. England's largest battleship (indeed the largest in the world), **Hood**, has been blown out of the water by the German battleship **Bismarck** in a sea battle near Iceland.

The weather is beautiful and warm. The crops are growing in an almost spring-like way. In three or four days the good sun has conjured forth a wedding dress of white on most of the apple and cherry trees.

Monday, 26th May 1941

In the Wehrmacht reports of 24th May, it was announced that the heroes of Scapa Flow have not returned from their U-boat's foray into enemy territory.

Monday, 16th June 1941

I received a little parcel with some more cake from home. Miriam writes that little Eva has sent a letter and all is well with her: I am overjoyed at this news.

Sunday, 22nd June 1941

This morning Dr Goebbels read a statement from the Führer and Reich's Chancellor Adolf Hitler over the radio, stating that Germany is at war with Russia. One can see without difficulty that the whole globe is gradually being swallowed up by this inferno.

Thursday, 24th July 1941

On the 22nd July, according to Wehrmacht reports, Moscow was bombed for the first time by German Stukas, after the Russians had bombed Bucharest and Helsinki. The Stalin Line has long been broken through on all fronts and Smolensk is in German hands.

Tuesday, 12th August 1941

Operations in the east are proceeding according to plan. The last Wehrmacht reports announced that more than one million prisoners had been taken, that ten thousand aeroplanes had been destroyed, as well as countless weapons and munitions, numerous tanks and guns. Moscow is being systematically bombed.

According to radio announcements, last night Russian bombers penetrated to the outskirts of Berlin and dropped a few bombs in an uncoordinated attack.

Another transport of the sick with seventeen men has left our camp. We drove them to the camp at Kreuzsee. There it seemed to me that I was entering a special Jewish concentration camp.

Thursday, 14th August 1941

On Tuesday, 12th August a Gestapo commission visited us here in the camp. They asked me what I did and I replied 'I am the Unterführer.' In Block 2 there were sitting two sick men, eating their so-called breakfast. The Kommandant upbraided them that they were not out working in the yard and I saved the situation by saying that they had been working up till then and that they had asked me about having breakfast. The Commissar then said to me: 'You are the Unterführer here, yes? Then in future you will behave appropriately when in front of your superiors.'

'Yes,' I replied.

Saturday, 16th August 1941

Early today I again had the sad task of burying another corpse. The coffin lid was not completely on and I could see his face. What a terrible sight to see the blood that covered it. He was 35 years old.

16

A voice over the telephone loops me back four months, splicing space and time between the August heat of my room and the cool spring of my accident and Christopher Street. It is Julius Neuburger calling from early morning New York, interrupting the silence of my London lunchtime with the pull of the telephone's vocal cords.

'Charley,' he yawns. 'I have a proposition for you.'

'As long as it's not one of marriage,' I reply, perhaps too dryly for an American.

Julius side-steps this remark and says: 'There's a Modigliani nude that I want you to look at in an artist's colony called Safed in the Galilee.' This would sound like some coded greeting that spies might have used in Cold War films if you did not know of Julius or Israel's wealthy and secretive art collectors.

I reply, 'I've been there; several years ago now. I'm returning to New York in October. Can the nude wait until after that, as I am already planning to take Caroline and Christopher to Israel from there?'

'Yeah, I guess it can. Charley, I want you to be my eyes in Safed as I can't get there at the moment to see her in person. There are also certain things about her history that we can discuss when you're here.'

The last time I visited Safed was the spring day I drove through the most torrential downpour of rain that I had ever witnessed. It was no April shower, it was a Biblical flood. The Internet site for Safed begins: 'A divine presence seems to hover over the mountainous peaks of Safed, one of the four cities holy to Judaism.' New-age artists live in Safed now, side-by-side with Mercedes-driving businessmen and their satellite links. In the Talmud the town is called Tzefiya, and it hangs high in the Upper Galilee mountains, peering down on the Sea of Galilee on the plain below from two thousand seven hundred feet above sea level, while Nazareth with its high-rise flats clusters on another hillside to the south. The vast ring of hills, of which that holding Safed is but one bead in the necklace, dominates the plain. Safed's white, Arab-influenced houses form a mysterious settlement once famous for its scholars of the *Kabbala*, the Jewish study of mysticism and hidden meaning. The town had something of a Golden Age in the sixteenth and seventeenth centuries when learned rabbis and Kaballists lived and worked there.

While I have been reminiscing, Julius has been on another telephone, mumbling endearments to someone whose identity evades the transatlantic line's reach.

'Charley, gotta go. It's going to be a busy day in New York. I'll give you another call in a couple of weeks to firm things up,' he says.

I ring Deborah in her studio on Fournier Street and at first she seems slightly surprised to hear from me. It has been three weeks since we last met and I am beginning to wonder how long the passport will take.

'I have Christopher's alias, Deborah: we'll call him Lebrecht Rittershaus.'

'What sort of name is that?'

'It was my grandfather's. A long story. I want you to use it in the passport; I never knew who my grandfather was until the other day.'

'You're an international man of mystery, Charley. The passport's taking longer than I planned: the Germans keep their blanks very secure under lock and key. I made a Gauguin for a man at the Embassy. I called in a favour from him.'

'In some senses Christopher is a work of art. Fashioned by time, by an unknown hand, *circa* 1920. Provenance unclear, turned up in New York in a street market, but European in origin. Nice patina, slightly worn. A good investment for any discerning collector of people.'

'I'm looking forward to meeting him. First I have to get his passport finished. When was your grandfather born?'

'10th February 1911. I found this out from the pre-1918 German census records. Even in Germany the name Lebrecht isn't so common.'

'How's it spelt?'

'L-E-B-R-E-C-H-T R-I-T-T-E-R-S-H-A-U-S. His first name means 'live right' or 'live justly'.'

'And did he?'

'Who knows, but I doubt it, given his record. He was with my mother's aunt until she died, then had a fling with my mother's mother, got her pregnant and went west to America. He disappeared and my mother never met him. There, that's the potted history of the Bernstein-Blanks. You know the rest.'

'Charley, I'm sure Christopher will make a perfect stand-in for your grandfather. He sounds sweet.'

'He's a man touched by tragedy and I want to help him. What I know about my past is like walking into a lumber-room full of valises, trunks, suitcases and bags that are lying around scattered and in disarray. You see a name on one and open it and find it empty, breathing out the musty smell of history. Others are stuffed with miscellaneous odds and ends that lead you down blind alleys. Then, suddenly, you open one small case and find a doll that belonged to your mother when she was a child. Well, for Christopher, his past is an empty room. Ever since I met him, I've wanted to try to help him to furnish it with something.'

'The empty room's a good metaphor, Charley. You should use it in your book. I can understand why you want to take Christopher under your wing. A loss like Christopher's isn't something anyone likes to see. That's what convinced me to help you help him. Let's hope your getting Christopher here changes something for him, makes something positive happen.'

'I won't forget this, Deborah. How long do you think the passport will take now?'

'Give me another week: I've got a restoration job to do for the Tate, but I'll have that finished in a day or two, then I can concentrate on Christopher again.'

'Will you give me a ring when it's done?'

'Charley, don't worry. You're fetching Christopher in October, aren't you? And it's only the end of August.'

When I return to Cambridge on the first night of September, there is a full moon so bright that it looks like a neat bullet hole punched through the black cloth of the night sky.

I walk to our house down the back alley that leads to the narrow garden. Caroline is sitting in a deck chair under the artificial sun of the security light, fixed to the wall above the french doors that open from the kitchen, and is reading with her head bent forward in concentration, her blonde hair gleaming in the harsh light. She hears my footsteps and turns to say hello, and as I lean down to kiss her neck I see that she is reading my translation of Isy's diary. I have never shown it to anyone before.

'Where did you find my manuscript, darling? I didn't know that I'd left it around.'

'You didn't. I wanted to know what you get up to when I'm not watching, what this book of yours is like.'

'You're as sly as a fox, I'll give you that. What do you think?'

'These diary sections are a little dry,' she says. 'You'd have thought Isy would have had more excitement to report than details of his correspondence: it's like reading memos from a labour camp. I guess he didn't do much while he was there.'

'Caroline, he was the *Unterführer*. I'm not quite sure what you'd call that in English: perhaps the 'vice-leader'. He wasn't writing the diary for a reader who needs polished prose and plot and mounting tension. He was writing it for himself, so as not to forget the details of what he saw and did. He already knew the emotions behind what he experienced each day in Sternberg. For him, the emotion – the drama if you like – was an implicit fact and did not need elaborating upon, if you see what I mean. That's why the diary's perhaps a little plain. For me, though, it's a minor miracle to hold it in my hands. Think of the journey it's been on. It's a real survivor: God knows there were few enough of them from the camps, and less and less as the years go by.'

'I suppose what he writes is a little like how artists talk about what they do. All they ever want to discuss, it seems to me, is the process of painting or drawing and the materials they use: the things that are basically outside their work, outside the meaning of the artefacts they create. They're never comfortable trying to explain the things inside their work, like the importance of their images. That's left to the viewer to figure out,' Caroline says as we head into the warmth of the house.

'It's not a connection I'd have made, but perhaps you're right,' I reply. 'In any case, I wish you'd asked me first before reading it. I wasn't ready to show it to anyone yet. In a strange sense, it all feels too raw still. Isy's words, I mean.'

'You can make supper tonight, that'll take your mind off it, my precious one. You'll find the raw ingredients in the fridge, Charley,' Caroline says.

As I prepare our evening meal, while Caroline is upstairs resting from her long day in the faculty, I hear Isy's words coming through the static. They are rancid whispers from my twin. He leans over my shoulder and breathes them hoarsely into my ear. It has been months since I last heard Julian's whisper. Like a mimic he has adopted a different voice, one that I can understand. He sings new variations on age-old themes, dances ahead of me to ragged tunes. Tonight he bewitches me, lures me into himself, threatens to win me over when I am at my most tired of fighting. If Isy is the protection that I hold up to ward off Julian, my twin has shot below my guard like a bullet fired low into the pit of my stomach, making a slow but fatal wound. I need a drink. Caroline could never understand.

... we behaved a little like animals when the food was distributed ... we must burn them at night ... we could freeze to death ... that man's shoulders and armpits are full of sores, he moans in pain day and night ... we are not allowed to leave the barbed-wire enclosure around us ... whosoever goes against these orders, or behaves contrary to them, will be punished ...

17

During my mother's last months, I watched her try to eat. Even a tangerine would make her vomit moments later into a bucket, the fruit mixed with clotted blood like some exotic cocktail. Eva's Sunset. As she could not eat, in the hospice she wrote down what she had been in her other life, as a child. I wish that I could feel it gave her some comfort.

> *Some nights I would wake up and see my mother standing at the window looking out and I would hear marching feet outside – the SS I suppose. I was filled with dread and often during this time when we were out for a walk I would hold my mother's hand tight.*
> *Eva Bernstein*

Just before her death, my mother said to me that she hoped she would see her mother, Miriam, again; hold her hand. For her last three months, she looked backwards into her life at what she had been. She took stock. Perhaps she recited her achievements to herself like some *curriculum vitae*:

Devoted wife to a talented artist for 30 years (excepting the five years of separation when he had his mid-life affair)
Mother of four healthy children (excepting the breakdowns amongst two of the four)
A-grade student (no money to go to university after the war, when nursing was the only government-funded course for a young woman with no family)
Fever-trained nurse for forty years (in between raising the four boys)
Some say I was a beautiful woman (later ravaged by disease)

My mother's qualifications were all qualified, like everyone's, I guess.

I never have visitors in my room on Conduit Street, or at least only one lately and he was looking for someone else. It is a bright September morning with that first sense of crispness in the air. The rush of traffic lulls me in the torpor that the commute throws over me like a caul.

I have only been at my desk for half an hour, looking through an art journal and drinking strong coffee to arouse me out of myself, when I hear the sound of footsteps on the stairs. At first I assume that they must be bound for the business that has re-opened below me after the summer break, but they continue upwards; sharp, high-heeled footsteps. It is Deborah, in a suit that makes her look like a commute-weary businesswoman. She explains that she is on her way to a meeting at the Tate and needs to look smarter than her usual studio uniform of smock and faded jeans. She takes out a brown envelope from her briefcase, which I notice is flecked with a constellation of minute white paint spots, and hands it to me with an expectant smile. I open it and see what I hope to see: the cherry-coloured covers of a German-European Union passport, with its legend *Europäische Gemeinschaft/Bundesrepublik Deutschland/ REISEPASS* and its crest of an eagle. I leaf through its fresh pages to the back and see Christopher's photograph, cut out of the only context that he knows and the only one, I suddenly realise, in which I have ever known him.

Beside the photograph it says: '*Name: Rittershaus/Vornamen:*

Lebrecht/Geburtsort: Wuppertal-Elberfeld/Geburtstag 10. Februar 1911/Staatangehörigkeit: Deutsch'. The red customs stamp on one of its blank pages reads *US Immigration NYC Admitted Sep 16 1999 for 90 days*. It is a wonderful original. Christopher looks ten years young for Lebrecht's years.

'Deborah, it's amazing. No one could tell whether it's real or not. You've done an unbelievable job,' I say.

'Believable, Charley. I hope it's a believable job. Actually, most of it is real as you know. It's just Christopher and the facts that aren't. Well, the facts in conjunction with him in any case,' she replies.

'I hope this will help him find out something real about himself,' I say as Deborah turns back to the stairs. 'That favour you asked for: I'd be happy to help if I can,' I add as she begins the descent.

I wait until late afternoon London time to speak to Christopher, knowing that the night and early mornings are when his stranding in himself is most complete, and when he finds it hardest to talk. His voice seems far away now and the Atlantic as wide as the gulf in his memory. It has been almost five months since we last saw each other and the same number of weeks since we spoke. I want to surprise him with the passport when Caroline and I arrive in New York. I want to give him this present and the path to his past that it might represent, without him knowing about it ahead of time. The first thing that he asks is: 'Tcharley, when are you coming to see me? Nurse Kowalski and I miss you.'

'In a month's time, Christopher. We'll be able to see you every day in New York. There's something I want to give you when we're there.'

'Is it something that's good; something that will help me, Tcharley?'

'I think so. I hope so.'

'Tcharley, life between the four walls of our room is no life. Nurse Kowalski says that I need to stretch my legs: I have been going for walks with her around the neighbourhood. I have seen many big cities on the television since I began again, but I find it hard to explain what seeing all the life in New York does to me. My therapist says that it will take me some time to get used to it, with my age and my difficulties.'

This is the most that Christopher has ever said to me in one breath and I am shocked by his rare fluency. Perhaps he is slowly beginning to wake up into whoever he was. I reply: 'I think that everything's going to be all right, Christopher. We'll take you out when we're there and you can explore the city with us. We'll keep you safe from harm.'

'I know you will try, Tcharley,' Christopher says. 'I often feel that harm has already found me.'

In preparation for my journey to Safed to see the Modigliani nude, I have been looking at his eyes, or rather the eyes of the people he painted. They have an otherworldly quality that no other modern artist has ever matched; they seem to be looking inwards, heavenwards. The eyes in Modigliani's portraits are not windows onto the soul, nor are they mirrors. They are filled with sky-blue nothingness. They have no pupils: they do not watch you, they watch themselves. There is no desire, no longing there. If you could step through his sitters' eyes you would find yourself where my mother went when she died: in oblivion or blissful peace. This nothingness is the key to Modigliani's portraits: his nudes' elongated necks and bodies and their supple limbs, the furniture upon which they recline or sit and the rooms in which they breathe, are conjured out of it.

Modigliani was a Sephardic Jew from Livorno, a beautiful, womanising alcoholic who saw sky-blue heaven in a cloud of hashish smoke. Perhaps he even dabbled in the *Kabbala*.

Blue eyes, green eyes. Modigliani's ethereal emptiness and the dying light from my mother's eyes the colour of green pools. They follow you, those eyes, and will not let you go. Both empty onto the unknown in their different ways. I held my mother's hand as she lay dying, blood clots welling up beneath the surface of the skin on her face and her mind already elsewhere. The words she spoke in her last days came out of the ether, out of the blue, out of the wild static of misfiring synapses as her spirit let go.

PART II

*'It must always get darker
before it can get light again...'*

18

Caroline has slept for most of the Atlantic crossing, waking up somewhere over Nova Scotia, Newfoundland, or one of those lonely islands that are only noticed by the in-flight navigation system. The image that I keep seeing on the screen is of all the journeys across this ocean that I have been on; the parabolic traces that they pay out behind themselves are like stitches suturing up a wound.

John F. Kennedy airport in the October rain. The man controlling the taxi queue is a yellow beacon in a fisherman's thick sou'wester, and we line up at his order to wait our turn as the taxis pull up and pull away again with their hauls. When ours arrives, I tell the driver to take us to the Manhasset Hospital on York Avenue, with a detour first to the Upper West Side and the two hotel rooms that I have booked for the night. Our itinerary is tight and the taxi kerb-crawls pedestrians in Queens in the early morning rush hour. Caroline rummages in her handbag, pulling out a lipstick and a compact, then puckers her lips and applies the pink gloss, checks her eyelashes and brows, flashes her teeth and looks into the whites of her eyes. I feel crumpled and cramped from the flight and anxious to see how the next days' events will unfold.

As we approach Manhattan, the high-rises and skyscrapers, the neon signs and advertising hoardings, the brown arc of the East River and the knife-straight lines of the avenues and streets roll out before us on this dark morning. The city cowers under great barrage balloons of grey and black cloud that release wave after wave of rain. When we get to the brownstone hotel, Caroline waits in the car while I wrestle the bags up the steps and into the lobby.

'Good morning, my name is Charley Bernstein. I have a double room booked for tonight under my name and a single under the name Lebrecht Rittershaus.'

'Good morning, sir. Welcome. Just a moment ...' (the receptionist, wearing a maroon waistcoat, a badge saying *Duane Edgerton* and a moustache saying more, searches the room cards). 'Here we go. Mr Charles Bernstein and Ms Caroline Field. And Mr Libreckt Riddershouse. A party of three. Tonight only, rooms one-forty-eight and one-fifty-two. Departure at ten ay-em. Can I see your passport for security please, sir?' (I hand it to him and he flicks through it while looking at me). 'That's fine, sir. Please follow me.' This being a small hotel, Duane doubles up as the bellhop. He takes me up to the first floor and opens the door to our room, sweeping me into a kingdom of fire-proof carpets and Formica. Christopher's first experience of a hotel will be a step down from the Manhasset Hospital, and the New York public hospital system is not for the weak or the insured.

I tip Duane a palm full of loose change – dimes, quarters, pennies – and head back out to the car and Caroline. The taxi driver nods in the rear-view mirror and the tyres unzip the wet tarmac. We cross Central Park on 97th Street Transverse and the rude interruption of nature to this stream-of-consciousness babble of concrete and asphalt, girders and glass, this hubbub of car horns and footfalls, of shouts and whispered echoes, shocks me again. The snow of February has turned to standing puddles and pools pocked by rain, water that deliquesces the earth, the mud on which this city is built. Water sips, licks, guzzles at the city's foundations, makes them unsure of themselves.

The 1930s façade of the Manhasset Hospital rises up like a cliff. Perched on the top where the braver rambler might lean, peering down into the abyss towards the street and its scuttling life, are masts and antennae that receive and transmit radio waves, rippling ever outwards to the limits of the universe, ever inwards towards the centre of things. The frequencies cut through the static and are themselves static. Some are channelled into the television in the nurses' staffroom on the Fourteenth Floor, slaking Christopher's thirst for knowledge. Others transmit information about new arrivals and DOAs, all-clears and autopsies. They tell us about life and death, if only we care to listen. Most of the people shuffling back and forth outside the entrance, sucking on the short fuses of their cigarettes, do not want to know the details. Only Christopher needs to know every last thing.

The taxi does a U-turn into a No Stopping Zone on York Avenue, stopping outside the door of the hospital. Caroline levers herself out on the kerb side, while I play chicken in the bus lane. The taxi driver, whose name 'Monplaisir' suits him poorly, hardly acknowledges the five bucks tip that I press into his hand. His yellow mass moves out into the tide of traffic and is gone downstream.

We announce ourselves at the hospital reception and rise in the elevator through the ranks of sickness and disease (First Floor: Oncology; Second Floor: Gastro-enterology; Third Floor: Cardiology...), arriving at the Fourteenth Floor: General Ward/Recuperation. It seems that the better you are, the higher you have to go.

Christopher is talking to a young nurse whom I do not recognise when we reach my old room. They both have their backs to the door; the nurse adjusting the window blinds at the foot of his bed and Christopher sitting on a chair, turned towards her. Christopher knows what is beyond the high windows now: he has seen it, walked it, tasted it, breathed it in. It is all a question of perspective: fear of the unknown or the freedom of it. The unknown can be a gentle walk through an unexplored valley if you have experience to measure it against. If, like Christopher, you have none it can be a plummet through a void. He had never seen or felt anything like the city before, he told me on the telephone. I said that he must have, in his other life. '... and I'm having two visitors from London today. They're very important in my story,' I hear Christopher saying like an eager child as we frame ourselves in the doorway.

'We've brought the weather with us,' Caroline's voice sings out. They both look round as soon as she has begun to say these words, the nurse with blank surprise and Christopher with a look of unadulterated relief and joy.

'Tcharley! Caroline! It is so good to see you. Nurse Liani and I were just talking about you, and now you're here.'

'Yes, we popped up in the elevator. Hello, Christopher!' (I hug him and Caroline kisses him on both rough cheeks.) 'Good to meet you,' I say to Nurse Liani. 'It's strange to be back in this room.' The nurse smiles and makes her excuses, then squeaks off down the corridor in her sensible shoes.

'So, you look well,' Caroline says. 'The New York air must be doing you good.'

'Yes, since I started my walks with Nurse Kowalski I have had more hope. But still no news, no news,' he repeats with a rheumy smile. 'Anyway, perhaps that will change now,' he adds.

Christopher has grown a short beard since I last saw him and this, combined with his white hair that is lit from behind by the windows, makes him emerge from the light like a saint in stained glass. Stained glass is more than the sum of its parts. It sheds a spectral light on those near it and is shattered by the slightest violence. Christopher is just a trick of the light.

After I have fetched three cups of coffee from the drinks-dispenser on the next floor, and while Caroline and I sip ours in a silence born of jetlag and the hush of the hospital, Christopher takes his old-fashioned cut-throat razor and shaving foam to the bathrooms on the Fourteen Floor. He returns clean-shaven and thinner faced; there is a Slavic slant to his cheekbones now. His blue eyes are hooded with heavier lids than before and his face has the look of an old child haunted by visions that only he can see. Caroline says: 'You look great, Christopher. We're taking you out for supper tonight, but first we're going to take you shopping to buy some new clothes.'

'That is so kind, Caroline. I don't have much, as you see.'

I look around this bare white room and realise that there is little for Christopher to take with him. It is as if his time here has left no trace. There is an alarm clock belonging to the hospital, the wristwatch that he was wearing when he came to on the side table by his bed, a book on memory that his therapist must have given him, and the trousers, jumpers, vests and underwear on his open shelves that the hospital administration has found for him. These are his only material possessions in the world, as far as he or anyone else knows.

When he is ready, having put on his watch and made his bed, we say goodbye to the nurses in the staff-room (Nurse Kowalski is on maternity leave) and ride the reverse-thrust of the elevator back down to earth. Christopher smiles and his blue eyes dart from me to Caroline, from the other passengers to the buttons indicating the floor levels that glow in descending order as we re-emerge into the world. As we wait for a taxi on the pavement outside the hospital, patients – some wheeling drips on stands, others with oxygen in tanks and masks on their faces – walk up and down in the lobby and on the pavement outside. They show us how the body also forgets: loses its memory for healthy order, misunderstands itself.

A yellow cab pulls up to the kerb, conjured by my sleight-of-hand, and we head further up the Upper East Side to Julius's gallery. It is high up on East 98th Street, where the bouffant-haired, wasp-waisted heiresses staggering with lapdogs under their arms slowly give way to an edgier type of character – shop-women, wide-guys, street-girls – as the city swells and crashes like a wave towards Harlem. It is still fashionably smart but the rent is cheaper.

Julius is with a client when our taxi pulls up outside the gallery and, as the rain has turned by the early afternoon to only a misty drizzle, we wait outside and show Christopher the works on display in the windows. Julius sells a version of taste. He sells it to shipping magnates, rock stars, media moguls, cosmetic surgeons, who have reached the pinnacles of their careers and have the money to spend on trinkets for their houses in the Hamptons. They do not know what to like or what to match with their silk-upholstered furniture, their gold lamps, and this is where Julius steps in with his tasselled loafers. Julius's gallery tastes are not my tastes. He sells mostly nineteenth-century paintings and drawings depicting *odalisques*, or women carrying jugs of water – often with one arm holding the high-necked brass water-jug to a slender, brown shoulder – and animal portraits. These works are not where Julius's passions lie, however: they just sell well and often and give him the money to buy modern art and to broker multi-million dollar art deals. Picasso, Matisse, Modigliani: these are the artists that he worships behind the scenes, whose works he keeps in his metal-walled room at the back of the gallery. The Modigliani in Safed might soon be getting a visa for New York, if its past is clean and I can prove it is authentic.

As we enter the gallery and step onto its ash-wood floors – the kind that make you feel that you are dirtying them with your shadow before you have even set foot over the threshold – the client is saying something about Berlin. 'See you at the art fair – there's a nice Gauguin doing the rounds, I hear,' are his parting words as he shuts the door behind him.

'He's a slime-ball,' Julius says by way of greeting. 'He sold me a fake knowing what it was. He just brought me my money back ... Welcome back to New York, Charley! This must be the lovely Caroline. Hello. And you're of course Christopher. We've never met.' He extends a manicured hand towards Christopher, who hesitates then shyly reciprocates with his own hand that looks as dry and fragile as a fallen leaf.

While Caroline walks around the gallery with Christopher, who glances indifferently at the works like a child who wants to be elsewhere, his face only lighting up when he turns towards Caroline, Julius and I discuss the Modigliani.

'The first thing that you gotta understand,' Julius says, 'is that the owner only bought it recently. He's in banking, I think, and I got to hear of him through a contact in Jerusalem. The man bought the nude in the early 1990s from a *princesse* in Paris whose family did something bad in Vichy France. I'm a bit worried that it might be one of our extractions; that it might come from a prewar Jewish collection. The woman in Paris said that she could not remember who her father had got it from. She did know that he paid about 800 francs for it, though.'

'Collectors always know what and how they paid,' I reply. 'Where and when sometimes escapes them.'

'That's kinda convenient for them and bad for us,' Julius says. 'I'm gonna talk to the guy again – he speaks good English – and see if he knows anything more about the painting. You'll have to do what you can when you're there and carry on back in London. Can you tell a genuine Modi from a fake, Charley?'

'It's all in the eyes, Julius. The sitters' and the beholders'.'

'It's all in the provenance as well, right? If we can trace the work back to Modi's studio, it must be by him.'

'Theoretically, yes.'

Julius wears a uniform of check shirt, yellow tie, mustard cords and dog-toothed hunting jacket – an outfit of the English upper classes topped by a dark, Russian-Jewish face. Pogroms and the political oppression in Soviet Russia forced his parents to leave St Petersburg, exchanging them for the cold eyes of the Ellis Island immigration officials and the cold shoulder of the Depression. History deposited Julius in the Upper East Side, dressing him as an English aristocrat.

We leave the gallery and begin our walk down towards Midtown, going against the current through the swell of the crowds on First Avenue. We are walking three abreast, Caroline and I either side of Christopher with our arms linked through his. Christopher says suddenly, 'I want to show you my city.'

Caroline laughs, 'You're quite the man about town, aren't you, Christopher!' and I add, 'We'd better try to find you some new clothes before you give us your tour.'

We go to some of the clothing stores on Lexington Avenue and kit Christopher out with a teenager's uniform of new jeans, T-shirts and jumpers; a septuagenarian in the clothes of a seventeen-year-old, in the American style.

By five o'clock, with the sky as black and shiny as indelible ink, Christopher has shown us where he sometimes stops for coffee and cake, a Polish diner on the corner of East 56th and Third, and taken us to his favourite bench in Central Park near the zoo. We talk about his walks around the Upper East Side with his therapist and Nurse Kowalski and I realise again that, unlike all of the old people I have ever known, Christopher cannot reminisce. He can look back on little more than one year of life, perhaps a seventy-fifth of who he is. The city is his memory; its topography maps his existence since he awoke. New York is his abridged biography. He says suddenly, looking at us with a gentle smile, 'I often wonder if I was ever married; whether I had a family of my own.'

We eat supper in Big Chill Burgers on West 68th Street. The ketchup and mustard bottles rise up from the tabletop like luminous plastic skyscrapers and I arrange street grids around them out of our three sets of cutlery while we wait for our food. We are all mute with tiredness after our long walk through the city.

Later, when we have finished our coffees and I have paid the bill, I take the brown envelope with Christopher's passport out of my bag. I push it across the table towards his hands and say, 'Here's the present that I promised you when we spoke on the phone.'

Christopher slides the passport out of the envelope and turns it over in his hands. He lifts his glasses and bends his head down to look more closely at the cover decorated with its spread eagle with outstretched talons, then flicks through its pages to find out who it belongs to.

'This is my photograph, Tcharley!' His eyes widen with surprise and his pale lips tremble slightly. He turns towards Caroline then back to me, wanting to understand.

'Who is Lebrecht Rittershaus?' he asks.

'Christopher, I hope you don't mind, but I gave you my grandfather's name and details. He came to America from Germany in the early 1930s and disappeared. You've found yourself in him, temporarily.'

'We're leaving in the morning for Israel, then flying back to

London from there in a week's time. I've got your plane tickets in my handbag: you're coming with us, Christopher!' Caroline says.

'Tcharley, Caroline, I cannot believe it. Are you sure that I can come? If they knew who I was, the authorities would never let me.'

'Don't worry; this way everything will be all right. You're staying with us in a hotel tonight and we're flying off early tomorrow.'

'But I haven't said goodbye to Nurse Kowalski or the others,' Christopher says.

'I think they'll understand. We'll ring the hospital from Tel Aviv,' I reply.

Once we have settled Christopher into his room and tried to calm him after the excitement of the day, Caroline and I slip between the nylon sheets of our bed by ten, before the wake-up call at dawn. It comes deep in one of my regular dreams. My twin is warning me of something that I cannot hear or understand. The sharp call of the telephone is a tocsin. *Never send to know for whom the bell tolls; it tolls for thee.*

I hurry to get dressed, waking Caroline with an instant coffee. Christopher is already up when I knock on his door. The window blinds in his room are raised, revealing a sky as black as pitch and the silent buildings across the street. His room is a *chiaroscuro* of dark shadows at its extremities and a jaundiced light from the two low-watt bulbs hanging from the centre of the ceiling, which illuminate Christopher as he sits on his neatly made, narrow bed, holding his new clothes in a large carrier bag from one of the chain stores. 'Tcharley, I didn't want to disturb it. I tried to sleep on the top,' he says to me. 'I had to wash myself in the sink; I couldn't get the bath to work. When are we leaving?'

'Caroline is just getting ready, then we'll find a cab. We need to be at the airport by six-thirty at the latest,' I reply. I am still numb with sleep and surprised again at Christopher's brightness so early in the day. When we shared our room in the Manhasset Hospital, Christopher was always up by dawn, as if he was a creature of nature rather than a twentieth-century man tuned to the clock on the wall.

He tried not to wake me, but with the discomfort that my legs caused I was a light sleeper and watched him mutely from my bed, between the raised casts and my journeys back into sleep and a world of broken dreams.

In Departures at JFK, we ask for a wheelchair for my grandfather: a vote of sympathy to ease our path through Check-In and Customs. We are flying American Airlines rather than El Al; they ask you fewer questions about who you are, where you have been and where and why you are going. No one recognises Christopher: the customs officials hardly give him a second glance. They never do when you are leaving.

19

Thursday, 21st August 1941

There was an argument about a parcel when the post was distributed today. Its owner became distrustful and did not want to accept it because the soap had been damaged and he wanted to ask his sister first, who had sent it to him, about this in writing before he would take it. I took this distrust personally and said that he would not get the package if he behaved like this. I spoke to the Kommandant and he said that I was correct in doing this. I distributed the few items of clothing in the parcel to the boys who were in need of them. It is strange how I always use the word 'boy' for young men who are almost married.

We have heard that our new Kommandant might be transferred to Minsk.

This morning I have already had trouble again. It is one of the sorest problems in our camp: that of finding shoes to wear. Today the weather is rainy and cool and the earth has been so softened through and through by the night rain that many with their half-rotten and destroyed shoes cannot walk to work. They stand barefoot and we have to try to find something, pieces of wood and the like, so that the men can be driven with force to the place of work. Some work on the spoil-heaps, others as brakemen and still others with the excavators. All the work is highly dangerous and alertness and precision are necessary to stay alive.

Monday, 25th August 1941

Today I went for the third time to a little lake nearby and cast fishing nets there. The weather was much too cold to go into the water; but I did go in, as I could not easily refuse. We did not catch much today.

Operations in the east are still going to plan. According to the last special announcements, the number of prisoners has risen to one million, two hundred and fifty thousand.

Saturday, 30th August 1941

The headline in **Der Angriff** announces: 'War flag over Reval.' The railway line from Moscow to St Petersburg has been crossed in several places. The Australian Prime Minister has resigned. Teheran has reported resistance.

Tuesday, 2nd September 1941

Today a new Kommandant took up his post in the camp. Early this morning I got into an unwanted and, for me, an unusually awkward situation. We were waiting to see the new Kommandant. The Gestapo and the Watch Commander had arrived shortly before; important visitors all round. It was feverishly busy. Upon the command to sweep out the so-called provisions block, which was right by the barracks for the team of guards (where the Watch Commander was at the time), I took a lad with me there. We had just finished when a guard opened the door and said that we had to leave immediately. I replied that my orders from the Kommandant were to sweep out the room. Answering him back at all was my mistake. The Kommandant himself then appeared and took a step towards me and we left straight away. I sat down for a second in the kitchens and the Kommandant called me over to the doorway where he was standing. 'The next time you are told to do something and you talk back, I will have you hanged in the middle of the yard, or from the fir trees that surround the camp.'

Yesterday, the 1st of September, marked the second anniversary of the war. If I think about what I have lived through during that time, I can only look at myself with surprise.

Tuesday, 23rd September 1941

As of the 19th September, every Jew in Germany has to wear a Yellow Star on the left breast with the word 'Jew' above it.

Friday, 3rd October 1941

The sun is shining; it is beautiful and warm. Only the mornings and nights are cold. When you look up at the clear autumn sky, when you gaze at night with awe at the wonderful starry heavens where Mars, Jupiter and Saturn are now the powerful rulers, you cannot believe that such violent slaughter is taking place in the east.

20

When Isy died, my brothers and I inherited the reparation money that the German government awarded him after the war for his time in the ghetto and the camps. Isy never touched the money, apart from a small amount to help my parents with my school fees, but chose instead to leave it growing exponentially like a benign tumour in the belly of the bank. I inherited my share when I was twenty and still at university. I bought a Swiss watch that I am wearing more than ten years later, a sturdy German rucksack, and a ticket around Europe by train with my closest friend from school. I kept the rest and I have spent most of it now on subsidising the rent of my London room. The final part has gone on our flights to Tel Aviv.

Christopher looks terrified on the flight. His wide eyes, open in equal parts of horror and wonder at the world, remind me of the face of my brother George's son when I took him on the rattling wooden roller-coaster at Coney Island during a family holiday to the States. Christopher sits across the aisle from me beside Caroline, as I am also scared of flying and think that she will be better at calming him. Whenever there is turbulence, I clutch at the armrests of my seat as if they are going to stave off disaster. I remember watching my mother do the same as a passenger in cars, grabbing the door-handle whenever my father swerved or swore, as if she wanted to eject.

The stewardesses make a fuss of Christopher once the aeroplane has reached its altitude and levelled out. They bring him a glass of champagne when we tell them that he is a first-time flyer, to congratulate him and ease his nerves. Secretly, Caroline and I realise that Christopher can now never know whether he has been in an aeroplane before. Perhaps he bombed the Wehrmacht as it advanced on Leningrad in the late summer of 1941. Perhaps he blitzed London or strafed the columns of survivors of Buchenwald as the Germans marched them away. To the passengers on this 777 he is simply an anonymous old man with white hair and a friendly smile; to the stewardesses he is my grandfather, who we are taking to meet a long-lost friend in Haifa, Israel.

Caroline talks to Christopher while I try to rest. We took off from JFK at 8 a.m. and, only a few hours into the eleven-hour flight, I am already tired by the early start and the prospect of the late arrival into Tel Aviv. Christopher knows where we are going; he has seen reports about Israel on the television, the stones and bullets of the *Intifada* and the ancient cities built on rock and sand. He calls it 'The place where your people come from, Tcharley,' and I reply that my people are actually from Łódz and London, Wuppertal and the West Country, everywhere and nowhere.

I will not cross the Atlantic again for a long time. I have neither the money nor the need, now that Christopher is no longer alone in New York. The business with Julius can be conducted by remote means: the electric storm of emails and faxes and the dangerous currents of surface mail and telephone conversation.

As we edge out over the scattered debris of islands, shards of tundra chipped off the old block of the north-east coast of North America, I think about how we mistake the sea for a watery waste, a desert devoid of life. It is all about surface to us; depths that we cannot see are no depths at all. Surfaces beguile us: we see a sheer granite wall and cannot get beyond it. We look at a painting's surface and cannot see behind it. There are lives that go on beneath all of these things. I wonder what goes on behind Christopher's eyes; beneath his fragile smile.

Our aeroplane opposes the trajectory of the sun. It rises in the west and touches down in the east, coming into a precarious landing at Tel Aviv. Caroline and Christopher stir from their mutual sleep and the Israeli passengers clap with relief and gratitude at a safe homecoming. It is after 2 a.m. local time, but my body does not know where its place in time is: I have gone from east to west to further east in the last two days, and I feel exhausted but wide awake.

Esta meets us once we have cleared customs; her kohl-black eyes reflect the humid night of the city. She is in her early thirties, like me, and has a young boy of three called Eli by a previous marriage. He nestles in sleep in the cradle of her arm as we search for her car amongst the clutter of taxis and buses and the crowd of late arrivals.

Her car is actually an ex-army Jeep and Christopher sits in the front passenger seat, holding Eli strapped into his lap as if Christopher himself were a human part of the vehicle's specifications, while Caroline and I ride crushed up in the back with the luggage beneath our feet. Eli and Christopher, the holder and the held: it is difficult to know which is which. Christopher looks down at the sleeping child as if staring at the sun, damaged by its beauty.

Thanks to her ex-husband's successful business interests, Esta's apartment is large, and thanks to her art historian's eye it is tastefully decorated and furnished. It is in a pre-1948 building, once owned by Arabs, near the beach to the north of the city on the road to Herzliya. Caroline and I have a room with a veranda overlooking the scrubby back garden, while Christopher has Eli's bright yellow-painted bedroom and is to sleep on an old-fashioned camp bed in there. Eli's cot-bed has been moved in with his mother and he runs around excitedly at the prospect of sleeping in the same room as her for once. He is a paradox on short little legs.

I have never seen Christopher looking so tired; he is the negative of health and vigour. His skin is translucent with age and the blue threads of his veins move with slow life beneath its surface, like underground springs in a winter landscape. He dabs at his eyes with a handkerchief, weeping out the effects of the aeroplane's air conditioning. He yawns and I say, 'Christopher, I think we all need to catch up on our beauty sleep. Your bed's ready.' All he can reply is, 'Thank you, Tcharley and Caroline.'

He yawns again and clasps his hands together, then shuffles from the sitting room to his bedroom down the hall.

Once he has gone, and while Caroline and I are getting ready for bed, she says, 'Charley, he's used to regularity, to the hospital. We need to make sure we give him structure and order. He'll go to pieces without it.'

'You're right, that's what I'm worried about as well,' I reply. 'I'm not sure that I've done the right thing by bringing him here. Perhaps he wasn't ready.'

'He couldn't stay in New York; he wasn't getting anywhere. At least with us he has the chance to find something, to become someone,' Caroline says.

'That's true, of course, but we'll have to keep an eye on him.'

'We will, Charley. Don't worry, we will,' she replies.

Before seven o'clock, Eli's young lungs have released their first cries of delight at the birth of a new day. I try to ignore the sounds of Esta preparing his breakfast and turn over, covering my head with a pillow. By eight, Caroline is pushing the cool flats of her feet against my calves and tickling my back with her sharp fingernails to let me know that she is awake. I roll over and kiss her once on her sleepy mouth, her long hair falling in the way like a velvet curtain or a waterfall, then climb out of bed and pull on some clothes. Christopher is already up when I go into the dining room to find Esta. He is sitting at the round table, drinking a cup of coffee and watching Eli slowly eat his slices of apple and bowl of cereal. Esta is singing quietly to herself in the kitchen and, as I say 'Good morning' to them all, she turns around and smiles through the hatch between the two rooms. Eli says in a quiet, sing-song voice, '*Sha-lom*,' and Christopher raises his cup and says, 'Little Eli here just taught me a new word: it's called *L'Chaim*. Esta says that it means "Cheers" or "To life". I feel that I have something to toast, being here I mean.'

Esta leans through the hatch and says, 'You do, Christopher, and there will be plenty more to celebrate for you, I'm sure.'

Caroline comes into the dining room in her dressing gown and ruffles Eli's hair, then stifles a latent yawn and stands behind Christopher's chair, placing her hands on his shoulders by way of greeting. He is wrapped in one of the thick, brown sweaters that we bought for him in New York, despite the brightness of the blue sky and the warmth of the late Israeli autumn outside the windows. He looks up at Caroline and smiles; I notice that he seems less exhausted than yesterday, although the burden of being haunted by an unseen past and beckoned by an unclear future still rests deep in his features, in the crow's-feet by his eyes and in the rich lines and crevices of the skin on his face; ancient maps that chart the forgotten emotions of his life.

Christopher suddenly says something to Caroline that pulls me out of my thoughts: 'Eli taught me a word and Esta told me its meaning. These are unexpected gifts. When are you and Tcharley going to start a family?'

Caroline blushes slightly at this *non sequitur* and comes round from behind Christopher, smiling softly at Eli again and coming to perch on my lap. She pours herself a steaming coffee from the pot.

'That partly depends on Charley, I think. Sometimes he's so wrapped up in the past that he doesn't think of the future,' she says, looking down at me and tugging my ear teasingly. Esta laughs and joins us at the table, then adds: 'That's the problem with these historian-types, Christopher: they're always dealing with the history of the dead, forgetting the here-and-now and the needs of the living.' She winks at me and laughs again, but there is also something serious in her eyes. Eli, infected by this apparent humour, giggles and claps his hands together, without knowing why.

21

Thursday, 16th October 1941

Yesterday, after a long silence, I received a letter from my sister Hedwig in Warsaw. Its contents amazed me, describing the reality of the situation there. She writes the following words: 'The people here fight with such a bitter despair over their daily bread that you often ask yourself where they find this last strength. From early morning until late at night, and often during the night itself, you hear their shouts and their cries, 'I am hungry: bread, destitution, death.' *In every street you see these poor people lying there crying; many swollen, many emaciated like skeletons. Only skin and bone – all from hunger. There are thousands of them ... Just as terrible as the hunger is this epidemic. The disease is called typhus and it persecutes people wherever they go. In every house there is at least one person with the fever and those that get it rarely recover. Often, when I see the high walls that cut us off from the so-called better people, a great yearning for freedom grips me. The world is so beautiful and so wide. Life could be wonderful if it were not for man and his hatred.'*

I also got a letter from home today. My sister Miriam has had to leave Wuppertal-Elberfeld and has taken a room in Barmen. She has heard that she might be evacuated with many other people to what used to be Poland.

I pray that this will not happen. It would be terrible, particularly after such a letter from my sister in Warsaw.

Miriam writes: 'Now we are each thrown back on ourselves and must carry on with our own strength. And if, in the future, we no longer hear from each other, dear Isy, we must go on with the aim of trying to stay united in our thoughts for one another.'

It is terrible, that thought of being left completely to your own devices. Are not most of us still small children who cannot walk on our own, but who should have learnt by now how to do so? Many will walk; many will fall.

Saturday, 25th October 1941

This afternoon I had a discussion with our **Kommandant***. It was about the Jewish race. He said, 'Speak your mind,' and asked me to sit down.*

'Must a Nazi by necessity have the prejudice that a Jew cannot be or become a human being?' I asked.

After a moment's silence he said, 'Of course!'

Sunday, 2nd November 1941

It seems that all Jews are being evacuated out of the Old Reich into the former Polish territories. Today I received a parcel from home with the news that Miriam was held back from a transport at the last moment and must now wait for the next one. She too must get through the greatest difficulty to come.

Tuesday, 11th November 1941

Another piece of painful news: my sister Miriam was transported with many others on the 10th November to the Litzmannstadt ghetto. 'A last greeting from home,' she writes. If you do not have the luck to be sent out of the ghetto to work, it is not much more than a vast home for lost souls who are beyond salvation. All those in the ghetto have neither an inner nor an outer home. They are led towards death by a blind guide.

Monday, 1st December 1941

I have just received a card in which I was told that my sister Miriam is no longer in the Litzmannstadt ghetto. Beyond that I have heard nothing of her fate.

Thursday, 11th December 1941

Yesterday I was told definitively that I had to hand over a death sentence signed by all of the Block Elders against Kraus, who had stolen eighty Reichsmarks. Further, I was to be made responsible for ensuring that the culprit either hanged himself by Sunday or, if not, would be hanged by our people on that day. Yesterday evening I met with the Block Elders and wrote: 'The Block Elders and the Unterführer of the camp Sternberg now sentence Kraus to death, as he has stolen eighty Reichsmarks from his comrades.' Today I gave this document, with all of the signatures on it, to our Kommandant and he said to me: 'You see, Bernstein, now I am pleased with you.'

Early on the morning of Monday, 8th December, at six o'clock, it was announced on the radio that Japan is at war with Great Britain and America. At midday today the Reichstag in Berlin met to accept a *declaration by the Reich's government.* The Führer, Adolf Hitler, announced that Germany and Italy would fight together with Japan against America. Today marks the first anniversary of our arrival in Sternberg.

Sunday, 1st February 1942

Either I have recently become ever more lazy in writing my diary entries, or the day-to-day events here seem to me too mundane. I have heard nothing from Miriam.

On Saturday the Führer gave a major speech to mark the day of his accession to power. From this speech can clearly be understood the future of the European Jewry. Even looked at by a Jew, the greatest tragedy is not that the Jewish race will be exterminated. What is most tragic is that in today's anti-Semitism there is this powerfully held prejudice that no Jew can be or become a good human being. This is the most significant and at the same time the most tragic thing: what they see as the evil of the Jews is not in their beliefs but in their blood.

22

The coast road from Tel Aviv to Haifa runs past Arab villages like patched-up rags on the backs of worn hillsides. Interspersed with them are Jewish villages and *kibbutzim*, whitewashed and pristinely ordered. We are packed into Esta's Jeep again, on the way to see Fishel in Haifa. She tells us that Israel does not allow the Arabs who live within its borders to modernise and develop their villages, deliberately making them build their homes on squalor and filth as if this would break their spirit. As buses explode with suicide bombers and silent young men move through the crowds in bars or restaurants to detonate themselves, the Jewish neighbours of Israeli Arabs realise that their neighbours are helping the Palestinian martyrs to get past the roadblocks and the blockades into Israel. Like loose cancer cells circulating in the lymphatic system or the blood, lodging in the brain, liver, or lungs, destruction comes from within.

This closing of the circle suddenly seems like a transgression. I am worried that Fishel might be reluctant to talk about his past when confronted by five people who are all relative or absolute strangers to him. I feel that I should have come to Haifa on my own and left my support-team behind in Tel Aviv. I could have travelled here on one of those famous exploding buses.

The gravel path to Fishel's apartment block on a leafy side street in Haifa, below the steps to the Bahai shrine on Mount Carmel with its golden dome that shines out over the city like a lighthouse for the soul, leads to an intricate wrought-iron door. I ring the doorbell for the third-floor apartment and a woman's voice says in a heavily accented English, '*Hullo, I wul let you een.*' It is Fishel's carer, Paulina, who has been brought over from his native Poland to look after him following the quadruple heart bypass that he survived almost one year ago now. His reparation money from the German government keeps him well cared for and secure in his extreme old age, looked after by the daughter of a Second World War Polish infantryman. He is able to speak to her in his mother tongue about his homeland and to tell her how it was before the war.

I lead the way up the concrete stairwell, with Caroline close behind me, followed by Esta holding Eli. Christopher brings up the rear, panting gently in his slow ascent of the three flights of steps. We arrive at Fishel's door and, as I am about to knock, it opens and he is standing in the doorway, wearing a shocking pink shirt with grey stripes, the shirt tails loose over the waist of his grey trousers. I am surprised by how frail he looks: history has a habit of making monuments of people and his thin body and head shrunk back on itself make him vulnerable and mortal, not the invincible survivor of the camps who strode through my childhood imagination. He has green-brown eyes like ripening hazelnuts: a hard surface, but with a soft kernel of goodness in them.

'*Shalom*. Welcome to Haifa and my home,' he says. 'You have the Bernsteins' eyes, Charley, and the hands of a writer,' he adds as we shake them in greeting. He leads us into the sitting room of the apartment and introduces himself to Caroline, Esta and Christopher; shakes little Eli's hand as he nestles shyly into the bosom of his mother.

Paulina, a dark-haired woman of about forty with deep brown eyes and a friendly smile, comes out of a bedroom and says, '*Hullo*, I am Paulina, Mr Rotstein's *cur* assistant.' 'I've heard a lot about you from Fishel,' I reply. 'It is nice to be able to put a face to a name, as us English say. You know, this is the first time I or any of my family now alive have ever met Fishel, after so many years of hearing stories from my mother about what he and my great-uncle did during the war.'

'Well, you can tell me what you've heard and I'll tell you whether it's true,' Fishel says with a shy laugh.

The apartment is simply furnished, with highly polished North African brass coffeepots and other ornaments hanging on the white walls. There are crocheted throws on the brown-upholstered furniture; windows running floor to ceiling dominate two sides of the main room, facing the burnt umber- and ochre-coloured blocks of flats nearby. Photographs of Fishel's two grown-up sons, now in their late forties and early fifties, and of his dead wife crowd the side-tables, cupboard-tops and shelves. Caroline says, 'How long have you lived in this apartment, Fishel?'

'Since 1953. My wife, Ruth, and I moved here from Tel Aviv after our first four years in Israel. We met in London, where I worked for three years after the war as an industrial physicist.'

'You told me when we spoke on the phone that you also worked for the power station on the road from Haifa to Tel Aviv,' Esta says.

'Yes, for many years I helped to set up and build the plant, which produces electricity for the whole of Israel. I wanted to do something that would help people and this was what I qualified to do as a young man in Poland. I studied at Kraków university,' Fishel says.

Eli struggles out of Esta's arms and runs around the apartment, giving us a commentary in his musical, high-pitched voice, a language whose intonation of inquisitiveness and wonder at the world I can understand, although the words themselves are foreign to me. He explores the unfamiliar topography of chair legs, the undersides of tables, the patterns of carpet and the grain of the wooden floor, hugs the pliant columns of our legs. The eyes of the two old men follow Eli with a fascination that only the old seem to have for the very young: an awe at their vitality and a benign jealousy of the life ahead of them.

Once we have finished the sweet black coffees that Paulina has made for us, Esta says that she will take Eli for a walk around the park and up to the Bahai shrine for the rest of the morning, so that Fishel can talk in peace.

He sits down at the dining table by one of the windows, with Caroline and Christopher either side of him and me opposite, facing the three of them as if I were in fact the interviewee. Fishel and I are perhaps three feet apart across the expanse of ivory damask tablecloth and the four placemats with their animal themes. He has his shirtsleeves pulled up, revealing the cobalt-blue tattoo *144115* on his left forearm, like a primitive barcode marking the cost of what he has lived through to tell me now. I ask what the small, finely wrought gold medallion hanging around his neck is and he unclasps its chain and passes it to me, silent but looking deep into my eyes like a man searching for some truth that he has waited his entire life to find. The medallion is a small gold plaque with the names of his parents and brothers and sisters who did not come back from the camps; the legend says, both in Hebrew and in English, *In memory of my family who perished in the Holocaust. My parents Moishe and Sheindl, my brothers and sisters Shimon Yoel, Isaac Leib, Samuel Aaron, Raisel and Freindl. Do not hate but do not forget.* I read the legend out in a hesitating, low voice to Caroline and Christopher, as Fishel mouths the names silently to himself like a mantra, over and over. It is all I can do to stop myself from crying, although Fishel's tears flow freely even after more than fifty years since his loss. He says that the pain gets worse, not better, as he faces his own mortality. I wonder whether he sees his brothers and sisters as old now, following him in age as Julian follows me, or whether they remain forever suspended in a dead time.

'I had been in the Łódz ghetto as well,' Fishel begins, 'but I did not know Isy there. It was not as simple as people think. There were thousands and thousands of people: anonymous crowds with only one or two friends. Everyone hated each other, because of the terrible crowding, the lack of food and the lice.'

'How long were you there?' I ask.

'From late '39 until '41. Then I was deported to a labour camp in

East Prussia called Pinnow; then to Sternberg in the spring of 1943. Isy was the *Unterführer* and six years older than me. I was very cautious about him at first.'

Caroline touches his arm and says, 'Yet he became your closest ally and friend?'

Fishel turns to his right to look at her with a soft smile and replies, 'Because we understood each other so well. I came from a small *shtetl* outside Łódz and Isy's parents came from the town itself; he still had some aunts and uncles living there when he grew up in Germany and they met again in the ghetto. We were both educated and shared our love of the arts and of people.'

Christopher watches us quietly, following our eyes and the movement of our hands as we talk. I realise that Fishel has said hardly one word to him since we arrived. Perhaps it is because Fishel lives in the past, in his memories, and Christopher is forced to exist day-to-day, so much in the present; trying to build a life of memory. Brown eyes looking back at what was and what has been; blue eyes staring at what is and what will be, unsure of what is in front of him.

'Did you believe in God in the camps?' Christopher suddenly asks.

Fishel turns to him, a look of deep concentration on his face. 'Charley has told me that you have lost your memory, Mr Street. It was like that with God for me: I forgot that he existed. I didn't see how he could,' he says.

'That is a little like how it is for me now,' Christopher replies.

'We heard in August 1943 that we would be leaving Sternberg for Poland; the Nazis were closing the camp,' Fishel continues, once Paulina has refilled our cups with coffee and brought us oat biscuits and some small, sweet round almond cakes. 'Baked by *Mistur Rotstein hum*self,' she says with a proud, motherly smile as he nods with a look of embarrassed modesty on his face.

'They're delicious,' Caroline says. Christopher and I echo her words with encouraging noises of chewing and swallowing.

'It was only when we got there, after a day and a night on a slow-moving train made up of goods wagons, that we realised where we were,' Fishel says. 'Many of us, or at least the Poles, of course already knew the name Oswiecim. The Nazis called this small, mud-soaked village "Auschwitz" and, even though we had been in ghettoes and camps, all on that transport knew by then what it was for. It was like you see in the films: the train went through that brick gatehouse with "*Arbeit macht frei*" above it and stopped at the platform where the selections took place. You know the rest; it has been repeated countless times for everyone to know. Worn thin with the telling. None of it can make you understand what it was actually like to be there, of course. But I'm sure all of you have the image in your mind.'

'I saw a black-and-white film of a camp once on the television at the hospital. I didn't really understand what it was until I asked Tcharley. I don't know the name of the one that I saw,' Christopher says quietly, his head bowed and his eyes turned towards the window.

'It could have been Auschwitz, Treblinka, Sobibor, Dachau, Mauthausen, Bergen-Belsen, or many others. The list is a long one,' Fishel replies, staring straight at me. 'When we got to Auschwitz, Isy and I had a terrible stomach sickness, what he called *Durchfall*. How do you say it in English? *Diarrhoea*?'

'Yes, that's it,' I interrupt.

'We needed something to clean ourselves with. It was the first evening there and us men from Sternberg, with others from different camps and towns who were the new arrivals and who had been selected off the trains to be kept alive, were in a vast brick building like a barracks. Everyone was crowded at one end and Isy and I went with another man to the other. Suddenly, I saw some folded paper on a beam high up in the rafters of the block and, by climbing onto Isy's shoulders, who stood, in turn, on this other man's shoulders – I never learnt his name – like an act you see in a circus, I managed to pull the paper down. And what do you think happened?'

'Everyone watched you cleaning yourselves?' Caroline asks timidly.

'No. They were not looking our way; only at each other. Wondering what was going to happen to them. I could not believe what did happen. To Isy and me, I mean. Almost twenty gold coins fell down on our heads like heavy rain. Someone had hidden them up there, wrapped safely in the paper that we were going to use to clean away the filth of our bodies. When I pulled the paper, they fell out.'

'A golden shower ...' I blurt out, before I realise what I am saying. Caroline stifles a smile by putting her hand over her mouth. Fishel seems neither to hear my comment nor to notice its effect on Caroline. Christopher looks from me to her and back again without comprehension, while I hide my embarrassment behind my raised coffee cup.

After a pause, during which he fumbles in a folder crammed with newspaper cuttings, old photographs and hand-written envelopes, Fishel continues: 'These coins kept Isy and me in extra soup for more than two months. I hid them by stitching them into the inside of the belt of my camp uniform. They were Wilhelm the Second twenty Marks pieces, like this.' He shows us a colour illustration cut out of an auction catalogue, depicting an egg-yolk-coloured gold coin adorned with the head of a man with a moustache, facing right. The text beneath the image reads: *20 Mark Goldstuck von Wilhelm II, Deutscher Kaiser, König von Preussen, 1897.* 'Isy kept trying to persuade me to get rid of them because they were so dangerous. I would have been shot immediately if they had been found on me. But I kept them as long as they lasted: this one for two extra bowls of thin soup with some root vegetables, that one for a new pair of shoes – when I say "new" I don't of course mean shop-bought! – and the other for the extraction of an infected tooth by the *Zahnarzt*, one of the dentists in our section of the camp. The gold helped save our lives. Even when we were both selected to go from Auschwitz I to work in Monowitz-Buna, where the rubber plant was, I kept the rest on me and they were never found. The extraordinary event of that first evening at Auschwitz, by a great *miracle* and a paradox, thus saved our lives.'

'I have always wanted to know what Isy did in Auschwitz to stay alive. Some people say it was pure luck or down to your age, your constitution or your fate. Others say that what you could do for the camp authorities made the difference,' I say, conscious of the tacit implication of Fishel in this question.

'We never saw the "authorities", as you call them, only their lackeys; their servants. The answer to your question, Charley, is very simple: Isy worked in a tailor's workshop in Auschwitz. In Wuppertal-Elberfeld he had been a *Herrenschneider*, a men's tailor. At least, that is, until he left for Switzerland. He made the camp uniforms that we wore from our first day there until our escape on the Death March. Once he found a gold watch in the pocket of a uniform he was repairing and, you will think this strange perhaps, I told him to give it in to the *Kapo*, to give himself a good name. This *Kapo* rewarded Isy with a week's extra rations: one bowl of soup more each day for seven days. And a packet of cigarettes that he kept and later swapped for extra food in the winter months of '43 to '44.'

Paulina comes back into the room from the small kitchen off the entrance hall and, bending down over Fishel's shoulder and smiling gently, says, 'I have pre*purd* some food for our midday meal, Mist*ur* Rotstein. *Shul* I serve it now?'

'Yes, thank you, Paulina, I think that we all need a rest from the past.'

She brings in a tray with a large bowl of steaming rice and a casserole dish of lamb stew, joining us at the table where we all eat in near silence. The food is simply prepared, but the strong flavours of cardamom and paprika give it a Middle Eastern accent that reminds me of how far I am from home. The shrill song of a bird that I do not recognise filters through the windows with the sunlight; the warmth of this autumn day, the womblike serenity of Fishel's apartment, makes our conversation and the cold Hell surrounded by its electrified barbed-wire fence that Fishel has conjured up seem so unreal. The foetid hallucinations of a man in his death throes, perhaps, or a nightmare dreamt up by Hieronymus Bosch.

As Paulina is clearing away the plates, Fishel begins again in a quiet voice, picking his teeth with a toothpick.

'After about a year there, I felt sure that there was a way to escape from Auschwitz. People are wrong when they imagine it was not so. But Isy could not speak Polish, so could not pretend to be a local, and the people in the villages around the camp would have known that he had escaped from there and killed him straight away. Those Polish peasants hated the Jews as much as the Nazis in Auschwitz. The chances of Isy surviving amongst the Poles were no better than staying where he was. I stayed with him for another six months after I had thought of escaping in July '44, before we were transported further into German territory, to Buchenwald near Weimar, in January '45. This was because the Russians were advancing through Poland by then; Auschwitz itself was liberated that bitter late January. We only stayed in Buchenwald for a little while and by that April we were on the Death March.'

'Buchenwald. *Beech wood*. A beautiful name for a place like that,' Christopher says, turning to look at Fishel with a haunted look in his eyes.

'*Sie sprechen Deutsch*, Mr Street?' Fishel asks.

'When I woke up in New York I could speak English, I think a little with an American accent, *fliessendes Deutsch* and Polish. I also knew some French. A man who specialises in accents came to see me at the Manhasset Hospital, but he said that I was the very first case he had seen whose birthplace he could not identify. He told me that I might be from somewhere near Gdansk in Poland; what the Germans used to call Danzig when they owned it. But he really was not sure: no one can tell me anything about where I come from.'

'The middle of Europe has changed hands so many times this century, like old coins going from one man to another and another. The coins get worn down and tarnished and the currencies confused, like when you have change in your pocket and find a coin that you cannot spend in the country you live in,' Fishel says. 'You have the sort of face I once knew, though. A familiar type of eyes: clear blue like the sky today,' he says, pointing out of the window.

'Now I must jump forward a little to the Death March, Charley. Esta will be back quite soon with Eli and there is too much to tell. *The bare bones, Fishel, the bare bones*, as my colleague in London, Mr John Perkins, used to say. We were being marched from a small camp called Langenstein, you understand that this was a small pendant camp of Buchenwald, in a very long line of hundreds and hundreds of men, all dressed in rags and camp uniforms, with bare feet or hobbling in broken shoes or clogs. We were walking though the Harz Mountains in our thin clothes and snow was blowing off the hills. It was *very* cold and the guards were beating anyone who stumbled, shooting those who fell. Isy and I suddenly saw a wagon pulled by horses being driven along the road by two German soldiers. It was carrying food. There was the sound of gunfire in the distance and these soldiers, and our guards, knew that the Allies were almost upon us. One of the guards suddenly shouted, "Run away!" I have often asked myself why, but I have no answer.'

'Perhaps because they knew they were beaten and wanted to try to help themselves by letting you go?' I ask.

'Perhaps, but I think not. Most of the rest of us marching in the freezing cold were killed by them with machine guns soon after,' Fishel replies. 'No one else seemed to be able to move, they were too tired and too used to their terrible inertia. I said to Isy that this was our only chance and that they would shoot us if we did not run right now and we ran like hell. It was now night, very dark, and the snow had turned to heavy rain. We were both wrapped in blankets and still wearing our Auschwitz clothes, you must remember. There was a deep ditch near us on the side of the road and we ran as fast as we could in our wooden shoes, crouching down low like animals, until we fell into this gully behind some rocks. It was very dark. The Germans were shooting after us, *bang, bang, bang*. The bullets came off the rocks nearby, but we were lucky. We lay down and then the shooting stopped. We waited and waited until the column of men had marched on and the soldiers in their cart had gone off, then we ran again into some woods nearby. After about ten minutes, we heard dogs barking and saw lights and the fence of a villa on private land. We lay on the ground in the wood and held each other to keep warm. I must have become unconscious for a short while; when I woke again there was more shooting in the distance and I saw an old man, a German Home Guard, standing over us with a gun.

'He asked very calmly, "What are you doing here?"

'Isy replied, "Nothing, sir, the SS have no food for us and have let us go."

'He could have shot us there and then, but he simply said, "Come with me," and took us to a shack with a stove burning logs. We were both freezing to death and as he talked we were not listening. I rubbed my hands together and I was shaking with cold. I made it seem even worse than it was so that this old man would pity me. He showed us a sack of sugar and said that we could take some to feed ourselves. I had not seen sugar for more than five years. We put our bare hands into the large sack, licked them over and over, put handfuls into our leaking pockets.

'Later, the old man took us to some German police stationed near the wood and one of these policemen gave each of us half a loaf of bread. The police said that they had no time for us; they must have been more worried about saving their own lives against the Russians. They had no time even to kill us. They told us to walk – on our own – to the local prison and showed us the way and sent us off. It was unbelievable. I thought to myself, "We have bread and sugar, we can survive," but we were still wearing our camp uniforms. As the dawn was breaking and we were walking along on the edge of some woods, Isy and I saw some locals working in the fields and begged them for trousers and shirts. The Allies were already in the area – tanks were now rolling past – and these Germans did not try to hurt us or to resist. They gave them to us and we wore our new clothes above our old wooden shoes.'

'Like a new life rising out of the old one,' I say.

'A little, yes, perhaps. But the old life was still near. A very young SS guard from the camps – he cannot have been more than twenty – walked up to us and pointed his rifle at us and said, "Halt!" but he was also starving thin and we gave him some of our sugar on a spoon that he was carrying with him. I said, "You can save our lives now; we will save you later," and asked him, in German, to take the bullets out of his rifle and he put them in his pocket. The three of us then walked for it must have been ten days. I cannot now remember exactly where we were or all of what happened: it was a very difficult time. One day we walked past an empty labour camp and some guards were still there. The Allies had not reached this small camp yet. We had not eaten for two days; all the sugar we had was used up or it had fallen from our pockets. We could only drink water from streams. These guards gave us food, but Isy and I did not trust them. We told them to change out of their uniforms and that we would defend them against the questions of the Russians and Americans when they came. They looked at us with a hatred; asked the young guard with us to stay behind, but he said *Nein, ich gehe mit diesen Leuten* and we walked on our way.'

'He was probably as frightened as you were,' Caroline says.

'He had more fear, I think. Although we were young men ourselves, in our thirties, we had survived Auschwitz and Buchenwald and knew what life and death were. He had only left home for the first time when he was conscripted to go to work as a guard in Bergen-Belsen in '44 and was sick, I mean that he *vomited*, when we asked him what he had seen. He would never tell us his name and still had the marks of acne on his face.'

As the sun sets, Eli stretches across Esta's lap with his back arched, sucking on his fingers. She strokes his soft hair while he hums himself quietly to sleep, tired after his games in the park beneath the Bahai shrine.

Paulina lights the Friday night candles as we gather around the table again. Eli sleeps beneath a blanket on the sofa and Fishel sings the *Kiddush*; his watery eyes reflect the candlelight as he holds up the cup of wine and takes a small sip. He passes the silver cup around and we each drink in turn; the wine is sweet and warm and tastes of life. Everyone is silent after the long day of conversation and we listen to the sound of cicadas on the lawns below the windows. I ask Fishel why my great-grandparents' graves in Wuppertal-Elberfeld might have still been intact at the end of the war and not destroyed by the Nazis. He says that he thinks it was because their graves were in one small corner of a mixed cemetery: there were not enough Jews to begin with in the town for them to have a cemetery all to themselves.

As Esta drives us back down to Tel Aviv, I think of the way that Fishel looked at Christopher for the last time before we left Haifa, still sniffing him with his eyes: needing to know what he had been in his life as a young man. *Friend or foe?* My mother did the same as a nurse in the treatment room of our local health centre when elderly Germans, Poles or Latvians came in to see her. Christopher would not know how to answer for what he had been.

The wheels sing their lullaby on the still-warm tarmac and Caroline, Christopher and Eli sleep in the back of the Jeep, while I sit beside Esta as she drives. The last thing that Fishel told me about the transport from Auschwitz to Buchenwald comes back to me: how he and Isy went from A to B in an open train in the freezing cold. Fishel found an old preserved food can and a length of string and tied the tin to the end of the string and dropped it out of the carriage, dragging it along in the snow and scooping some up to quench his and Isy's thirst. From A to B they passed through Czechoslovakia and stopped at a station. Locals on their way to work threw sandwiches and bread into the open wagons and Fishel caught a loaf of about one-and-a-half kilos and did not want the others in his wagon to see it. They would have killed him for it if they had. When it had become dark, Fishel carefully showed it to Isy and shared it with him. Fishel coughed while Isy ate, to disguise the sound of his chewing.

23

We are waiting in the early morning at Tel Aviv's central bus station for the bus that will take us down through the Negev desert to Eilat. Young conscripts in green uniforms, their rifles slung low over their shoulders, stand in clusters at bays for buses bound north for the Galilee, east to Jerusalem or south to the Dead Sea. The men and women are tanned caramel brown, with the dark hair and deep brown eyes of the Mediterranean; they look muscled and hardened, not like the pale, bookish Jews from Poland and Germany who made me part of what I am. The soldiers smoke, swapping jokes and stories as they wait.

Christopher looks around at the throng of people and asks, 'Do you feel at home here, Tcharley?'

'This is nearly as alien to me as New York was to you. I understand something of Fishel's past, but these peoples' present and future is a different world. They all seem so young and yet so hard.'

'They have to be,' Caroline says. 'Like Fishel, you grow up fast when your life's in danger.'

The bus is crowded with soldiers, *kibbutzniks*, tourists, and old men and women travelling back home to remote settlements. The passengers talk loudly as we leave Tel Aviv and pass through outlying villages and towns along the route; becoming more subdued as the bus descends from the plateau and the monotonous thrum of the desert begins. It surprises us with oases surrounding *kibbutzim* and settlements, where one or two passengers alight each time and birds of prey circle overhead, waiting to pick off the riches that the fertile ground offers up to them. For the rest, the landscape is like the surface of the moon with the heat turned up. I ask a young soldier behind me, 'Do we stop halfway for a break; to get some food?'

'Yes, in about half an hour. Where are you from?'

'I work in London and live in Cambridge, where the university is.'

'I know it; my cousin Joel went there. He studied philosophy. Are you Jewish?'

'I have never been sure; half and half, I suppose,' I reply. The heat mugs you as soon as you step out of the security of the air-conditioned bus. Christopher is silent as we sip our lemonades in the roadside café at the heart of the desert. He looks deep into his glass as if into another dimension, mesmerised by the ever-changing constellations of the juice's swirling pulp. Caroline stretches her arms and arches her back, half yawning and half smiling as she sits across the table from me.

'Are you all right, Christopher,' I ask. 'You seem quiet today.'

'I feel that the landscape is telling me something about myself. I am listening to what it has to say. It says that there are no trees, no animals; that there is no life.'

'But there is so much life here, Christopher,' Caroline says as she touches his arm. 'It's just that it's deeply hidden. People live out here in the desert; animals hide in their burrows and come out at night when it gets cooler. The birds feed off them. It's just often difficult to see the richness of the existence here; it's below the surface, out of sight.'

'That might be so. Still, today I feel very sad for myself,' he says.

We reach Eilat by the early afternoon and take a taxi to the house of one of Esta's friends, Shulamith, who is to put us up for the night until we travel on into Egypt, crossing the Sinai desert as far as St Catherine's monastery. The monastery nestles at the rocky foot of

Mount Sinai itself, where Moses received the Ten Commandments, and shrouds the most important collection of icons in the world in the silence of the mountain rock from which the great church is hewn. Some of these icons date as far back as the fifth century, and iconologists travel from all four corners of the earth to see them hanging in their twilight world. Caroline has read many academic papers about the icons and seen them reproduced in countless books, but this will be her first professional pilgrimage to the place itself.

Shulamith is in her late thirties, with that independence of spirit that I know from Esta. She is a painter who does actually wear a beret and smoke the *Gauloises* she has imported from France. Her studio is in the garden at the back of her house and she shows us around casually as soon as we arrive. The large wood-walled room is filled with vibrantly coloured abstract canvases covered with intricate patterns of splashed and dripped reds, oranges, greens and yellows; throwbacks to the Abstract Expressionism of Willem de Kooning and Jackson Pollock. Shulamith has a good technique, but technique is never enough. It is all in the soul of the work. The chaos and the maelstrom that the paintings conjure up remind me of Julian's voice coming through the static. '*It is all in the soul, Charley*,' my dead twin says, '*it is all in the soul.*'

I have never learnt to tell the truth to bad artists, choosing to lie to them about my thoughts when I feel that their work is ill-conceived, unoriginal or lacking in technique. As with most things in life, not confronting the truth from the outset in moments of weakness seems the easier path to follow, although I have learnt that it nearly always rebounds on you and that honesty would often be better, or at least less exhausting. In the case of foreign artists in a country lacking in the international fine-art markets that London or New York offer, showing a positive reaction to their work when there is none often encourages requests for help. 'They're interesting, spontaneous and free,' I venture, while Caroline looks on blankly, probably already dreaming of her icons, and Christopher stares out of the large windows at the garden.

'Do you know a good dealer in London, someone who can help me?' she asks.

'I'll have to have a think about it and let you know,' I reply.

While we are drinking iced tea on her veranda in the late afternoon, the sunlight playing its fingers down the spines of the tall trees on the perimeter of the lawn, we listen to the repetitive susurration of the water-sprinkler that keeps the grass green. Shulamith asks what we are going into Egypt – 'the land of the Arabs' as she calls it – to see.

'The famous icons in St Catherine's monastery. Back in England I specialise in icons, their meanings and their history,' Caroline replies. 'And, you know, they're images of the Christian faith in the middle of the desert in an Arab land. Many of them have been there for hundreds and hundreds of years, safe from all of these divides of faith and politics that everyone always talks about here.'

'We talk about them because they exist for us on a daily basis. People die for and because of them every day,' Shulamith says. 'You know, my seventeen-year-old nephew was killed only last year at a border checkpoint?' she asks.

'I am very sorry to hear that. I didn't know,' Caroline says. There is a long silence made all the heavier by the palpable sense of Shulamith's loss. Some children are playing football in the distance and the thudding sound of the ball as they kick it along a dusty street and their shouts of excitement are all that break the spell. I think of the divisions that a conversation about a visit to see some ancient icons, simple artefacts of faith, can provoke in the heat of the desert. The realities here are not about aesthetics: they are about belief, about blood. The desert is a harmonious continuum; the nature of its undulating harshness, of its life-giving oases and slow death, does not change from one country to another, yet the world seen within its individual grains of sand turns on its axis somehow.

'As an artist, you must believe that art transcends race, religion, the individual personality from which it springs; even the culture from which it comes,' I suddenly ask, breaking the silence.

'I try, but it is so hard. We have grown up with these things. They are part of us, of who we are,' she answers.

At four o'clock in the morning, Caroline, Christopher and I are standing at the bus stop where the coach for St Catherine's will pick us up. The curfew of the dark has yet to be lifted and the streets are like the grave, scrubbed clean of the living and thick with the voices of the dead whispering on the breeze. Caroline and I huddle together for warmth and Christopher wraps his coat tightly around his body, hugging himself with his arms.

When the coach arrives, it is half-full of wall-eyed American tourists who murmur over thermos flasks of coffee and point out of the windows blank with night, as if showing each other what nothingness looks like. We all try to sleep, Caroline leaning her warm head against my shoulder and Christopher in the far seat across the aisle, resting against the hard windowpane. By six o'clock, we have passed through the border control into the Taba Peninsular. Christopher, the fledgling tourist, now has an *A.R.E. Taba Peninsula Passport Valid for Aqaba Coastline* visa stamp to add to the one marking his fictitious arrival as my grandfather, Lebrecht, in New York and his real entry as someone else into Israel.

As the Egyptian sun rises, I think of the reverse of this journey three thousand years ago: how the Jews passed over from Egypt into the Promised Land. It all seems so simple and believable in the Old Testament and so undermined by the banality of the reality here: the reek of the border guard's cheap cigarettes; the naïve misspelling of 'peninsular' in the passport stamp; the fumbled silence of the other passengers on the bus on their Bible Tour.

The coach winds precariously up steep mountain-passes to lumber down sinuous roads that hug the edges of precipices until we reach the desert floor again. Bedouin children crowd the coach's doors every time we stop at lookout points to admire the early morning view before the breathtaking heat of the day clamps down on the landscape. The children try to sell us beads, necklaces, bracelets and uncut semi-precious stones – lapis lazuli, turquoise – that they have dug from the earth here. The American tourists say things like: 'Gee, look! These Arab kids sure've got a lotta things for sale!' but buy nothing before stumbling, stiff from the coach, to gape at the mountains and ask: 'Are we still in Is-*reel*?'

Caroline hands over some coins, a mixture of pence and shekels, for a piece of turquoise carved in the shape of a minute camel. The children smile shyly and nod their thanks, then clamour for sweets and chewing gum. They seem not to notice that the currency is no good to them, but I understand the transaction of which Caroline was a willing part when I see the strings of foreign coins like talismans that they all wear around their necks.

The Bedouin children shake Christopher's hands and look up at him from beneath their dark eyelashes as he climbs awkwardly onto the coach again. He waves slowly from the windows as we pull away, driving ever deeper into the desert towards Mount Sinai. 'Tcharley, you tell me that they live out here in the desert, sleeping in tents under the stars and moving from place to place. They seem so happy in their freedom.'

'Yes, I'm sure they are,' I reply. 'It's all that they know. If they lived in towns or cities, crowded together between buildings and concrete, I think that they'd die out as a people,' I reply.

An hour further along the desert road, its tarmac pocked with potholes that make the coach lurch from side to side, we suddenly pull over, drawing up onto the hard-baked sand where the coach is shaded by a group of stunted trees. 'Now we are going to visit an authentic *bed*-win *fam*-ilee in its tent and drink some teas with them,' the middle-aged man who is our tour guide announces in a thick Israeli-Arab accent. The Americans applaud this short speech and begin to shuffle carrier bags and backpacks, clicking open the shutters of cameras or switching on camcorders as we climb out into the oppressive heat.

The white tent is a short walk over the tall sand dunes. The adults and children of an extended Bedouin family sit beneath its shade, with the broad front wall rolled up and tied to the edge of the flat roof, exposing the interior and its occupants, who sit cross-legged on the bare sand. They watch us coming down their side of the dunes from a hundred yards away, the men smoking *shisha* pipes and drinking tea, while two women make unleavened bread on an old upturned oil-drum. A camel ruminates at one side of the tent while children play with sticks and stones in the dirt. The scene could be taken from the Bible if the oil drum and the anachronistic wristwatches that the family wear were edited out.

After our guide has greeted the family with *Salaam* and they have nodded and exchanged their news, an old friend who brings his tour group to visit them each week, perhaps, the women pass round a tray of pot-bellied glasses with sweet apple tea for us to try. Caroline and Christopher sip theirs quietly, sitting either side of me on the cushions that the Bedouins have provided for their Western guests. The smell of the wood-smoke from the primitive oven that baked the bread we now let cool on our laps mingles with the richness of the aromatic spices from the tea. I suddenly realise that I feel at peace for the first time since my accident in New York. I listen to the beautiful serenity of this ancient scene and all I can hear is silence.

The low wooden door of St Catherine's monastery is set into a sheer wall of vast blocks of stone that seems to grow out of the mountain rock itself. The wall forms one side of a steep road that leads from a car park with two restaurants and a gift shop. Apart from the monastery, this cluster of buildings is the only sign of civilisation for mile upon mile of desert. All around is the claustrophobia of emptiness.

We enter the labyrinth of corridors and passageways that leads through the monastery to the church, groping our way unsteadily in the half-light. Caroline, Christopher and I walk in single file, holding hands in a human chain and guiding one another. The lit bloom of the candles, held in ornate metal containers suspended on long brass chains from the great roof of the church high above our heads, is what I notice first. The islands of light that they create punctuate the darkness and cast a flickering aura over the walls, the black-and-white tiled floor and the pulpit. Ancient dark faces gradually rise from the walls against gilded backgrounds burnished with age. Caroline moves like a somnambulist from one icon to another, as if hypnotised by the rhythm of their eyes. Christopher stays close beside me, whispering over and over that he has never seen anything so beautiful.

These, then, are the faces of the dead. These are the faces of people no one has ever seen. St Matthew looks down at us myopically like a Talmudic scholar, backlit with radiant gold that shines out amidst the darkness. An icon-maker, perhaps working in Anatolia in the fourteenth century, shows St John framed by a mane of rabbinical white hair. Another from eleventh-century Kiev depicts St Mark wearing a lamb like a stole around his shoulders. Jesus Himself wears a tightly twirled black beard and raises his right hand in the sign of the Lord. He anoints us with his dark-rimmed eyes that remind me of Esta.

As we emerge back out into the light and the desert heat, Caroline squeezing my hand tightly with excitement and Christopher shielding his eyes against the midday glare, I cannot get the idea out of my mind that if any one of the men on the icons had been born, say, in Kraków or Berlin during the 1920s, they would have ended up in the ghetto or the camps.

24

Tuesday, 3rd March 1942

I have received a card from Warsaw: my sister Hedwig writes that she has heard that terrible things have happened in Łódz, and that, if our sister Miriam was there, she must now be lost beyond hope.

Friday, 29th May 1942

In East Asia, the Japanese are winning victory after victory. Nearly all of the archipelagos of islands in the Indian Ocean are in Japanese hands.
    My sister in Warsaw has sent me her love second-hand through someone else here.

Saturday, 13th June 1942

My diary entries are becoming, as I have noticed, ever more infrequent.

This year, summer does not seem to want to arrive. The weather is mostly cool and dry. You can almost feel the sluggishness of the plant growth. It is as if the powers of nature, in particular the sun itself, are at war with the earth.

For a long time I have not written anything about what is happening in the outside world. The Reich *of the 31st May 1942 reports: 'A German U-boat sank three ships in the St Lawrence River, increasing the number of vessels sunk in American waters ... During the ceremony on 20th May at the Reich's Chancellery to honour munitions workers and farmers, the first Knight's Cross was awarded to Hans Halme, the foreman of a munitions factory. Reich's Marshal Göring gave a great speech about the manufacture of Germany's armaments ... A state ceremony took place in the new Reich's Chancellery in the presence of the* Führer, *honouring the dead* Gauleiter *from the district of Weser-Ems ... In Frankfurt-am-Main, the Secretary of State Von Weizsäcker welcomed back onto German soil the diplomats from America ... The Head of the SS and Chief of German Police, Himmler, oversaw the swearing-in of the volunteers for the Dutch SS in The Hague on behalf of the* Führer *... The Caliph of Morocco met the Spanish Head of State, Franco, for an official visit in Spain ... In South Africa the imminent visit of Mrs Shiang-kai-shek is expected ...'*

Saturday, 20th June 1942

It is almost ten o'clock at night and I am still writing in good daylight. I can hear Russian songs sung by Ukrainian voices in the neighbouring barracks. In the camp there are now French, Russian, Ukrainian, Jewish, Polish, Dutch and German prisoners.

At long last I have received some more news of little Eva: Dr W. in Wuppertal-Elberfeld has heard from her and she sends her greetings to me. How I would love to be at home again.

Another man has died and been buried.

In the field of battle, General Field Marshal Rommel has almost reached Alexandria with his troops. In the newspaper it was announced yesterday that a convoy was blown out of the water in the Arctic Ocean. German troops are everywhere on the advance; some fourteen days ago Sebastopol fell, the strongest fortress on earth.

I have received no post from home for a long time now.

Monday, 21st September 1942

Early this morning one hundred and fifty-one men were transported from here back to Litzmannstadt.

Tuesday, 29th September 1942

The main problem that preoccupies us most particularly at the moment is death. Indeed, it preoccupies most people in wartime, but not so much – as with us – the manner of the death itself. We have not searched out this problem; rather, it comes to us each day, shuddering and mysterious, reminding and calling us.

Friday, 2nd October 1942

The day before yesterday the Führer gave a speech in which could be discerned a powerfully suggestive – even for the enemy – desire for victory. For us Jews it looks sad. It is sadder still that all Jews without exception belong to the species of 'criminal'. Is it not tragic that the Jewish race is the only people in the world amongst whom no exceptional people – let us say no relatively good people – can be found?

Thursday, 8th October 1942

Recently, cases of TB have been diagnosed ever more often and the patients are being transported back home.

In the theatre of war, Stalingrad is being fiercely fought for. One of this war's heaviest and most bloody battles is surely taking place there.

Wednesday, 28th October 1942, evening

Today marks the passing of four years since that day of 28th October 1938, so memorable for many people and for me, when we were transported out of our homeland into Poland. Four years of suffering. The thing that has moved ever more strongly into the foreground of the soul over those four years is the problem of death. Death has become ever better known to us.

Saturday, 21st November 1942

On the way to the railway I talked with B. about our fate as Jews. I said that it was more or less predetermined by the heavens and that these people could be seen as the tools for carrying out this fate. B. argued against this and said that it was too systematic-materialistic a view. On the way back, I let this run through my head again and it became clearer to me. Of course we were not put on the earth to die in a more or less cruel way.

Tuesday, 24th November 1942

A dear letter from Miriam in which she writes that we really did live through wonderful times together, but that today she would no longer *know where to begin with this 'family happiness'. She writes that she can no longer deviate from the path she now follows and that to her 'my brothers and sisters have the same goal in front of them'.*

25

After a day in Tel Aviv to allow Christopher to rest following our late-night return from Mount Sinai, Caroline writing up her thoughts and me writing down mine, we set off in the early morning on the fifth day of our week in Israel to travel up north to Safed. I have a headache from the desert sun; my heartbeat throbs in my temples and behind my eyes with a quiet insistence that a dose of codeine has not cured.

Esta is quiet as she drives, concentrating on the fast-moving tide of traffic around us. When she stops at traffic lights, she manoeuvres the Jeep as far as she can from any buses. 'In case of the suicide bombers,' she explains. Eli sings to himself in the back and Caroline and Christopher talk with excitement about our journey into Egypt.

'Tcharley told me that no one knows what anyone looked like before photography was invented. He says that the camera is objective and that the portrait painter always paints what he wants to see,' Christopher says.

'He's right, I suppose,' Caroline replies. 'People do say that the camera never lies. Sometimes when I look at photographs of myself, though, I think that it must do. I can't be *that* bad,' she laughs.

'The people who made the icons that you saw, Christopher, were working from a kind of template, a code: they didn't invent; they copied and adapted. They didn't claim to know, for instance, what Jesus looked like. That wasn't important to them,' I add. 'What was important was what He meant, what He said to them.'

'Charley, you talk about Him as though he existed,' Esta suddenly says. 'I thought that us Jews weren't meant to believe in Him.'

'Okay, so for those adults in the front of the Jeep He doesn't exist and for those in the back He does?' Caroline asks teasingly.

Once we have driven for about one-and-a-half hours up from Tel Aviv towards the Galilee, we stop at a roadside tent where a man and woman are selling pancakes. Esta tells us that they are Druze, members of a religious sect who broke away from Islam in the ninth century and whose beliefs and practices are kept secret from the outside world. The Druze people, she says, live in the Lebanon around Mount Hermon and in the mountains behind Beirut and Sidon. Their villages are also found on the Golan Heights and have landed like scree or fallen debris from higher up the slopes inside the northern border of Israel.

Time and the wind and rain of the more temperate climate in the north have etched the man's face: deep lines like ravines cut into its topography, fanning out from the brown wells of his eyes and trickling over his cheeks to converge around his mouth again. The woman, perhaps his wife, has been less eroded by space and time, but her clear green eyes are a shock against her dark brown skin and black hair.

The couple smile as we approach and the man squeezes lemon juice and shakes sugar onto the freshly made pancakes; a sudden flurry of weather on their desert surface. Christopher folds his pancake in on itself like a secret, wrapping his hands around it and eating in silence. Eli chews noisily and Esta wipes the lemon juice from his chin. The Druze couple wave as we go back to the Jeep: two ducts for manna from Heaven in a tent surrounded by wilderness, on a road streaked with the diesel-fumes of long-distance freight containers and short-haul tourist coaches.

We arrive in Safed towards lunchtime and Esta parks the Jeep at the foot of the steps that lead up to the heart of the old town. As we climb them, the view opens up over the gently undulating hills and valleys that lead for perhaps five miles towards the Sea of Galilee, what the Israelis themselves call Lake Kinneret. The autumn sun is weaker up here in the north, bathing the hills and their scrubby undergrowth in a light exhausted by the heat of the summer now past.

The Modigliani, a reclining red-haired nude from 1920, the last year of the painter's life, lives in an austere white villa surrounded by high white walls.

'*Shalom*?' a male voice says in a low, cigarette-soaked timbre when I press the intercom.

'This is Charley Bernstein. I have come on behalf of Julius Neuberger to meet Mr Cahane,' I reply.

'Please come in,' the voice says. 'He is waiting for you.' The heavy metal door swings open with the faint whine of a motor and we walk through a dark hallway into a cavernous room. Running down its centre is a long wooden table that must seat twenty people with ease. A tall man, perhaps fifty years old, is standing at the head of the table, with a younger, heavily built man beside him, wearing an open-necked shirt that exposes a mass of dark wiry hair and a gold chain. The older man is in an elegant white linen suit.

'Hello,' he says, 'I am Claude Cahane. This is my personal assistant, Zvi.'

Cahane's incisors are too long; they give him a rapacious look like a feral dog or an urbane vampire. Esta, who has spoken to him once on the telephone to arrange our visit, introduces herself again. He smiles at her without warmth and ruffles Eli's hair. Eli shrugs away his hand, burying his head in the bosom of his mother. Caroline and Christopher look around in silence at the overstated opulence of the villa; its owner seems not to notice them, while Zvi glances over in their direction as his master talks. 'Quite a gathering to see the painting,' Cahane says. 'Let's hope she's not shy.'

Zvi's muscles shake as he laughs with unsmiling eyes. 'She's not wearing much, as you will see,' he adds.

'She *is* a nude, isn't she?' I joke, trying to lighten the mood.

Cahane leads the way through from the dining room into a long sitting room, bathed in a warm light where we are standing and in almost complete darkness at the far end. Pale silk cushions are strewn like fat lotus blossoms across the Persian carpets and the walls are bare. A Mozart sonata washes out from unseen speakers. With a nod, Zvi disappears into another room and Cahane picks up a remote control. I wait for the sonata to stop, but the far end of the room is suddenly flooded by a harsh glare and on the wall, as if unclothed by the light, is the nude.

She is lying on her back on a divan, with her chin cupped by the fine fingers of her left hand that rises like a lily out of the marble-white stem of her arm. Her hair is a deep auburn, flowing down over her shoulders and covering her right breast. It is the absence of her eyes that is so compelling; there is a heavenly void where they should be, as if they have vaporised. It is the absence of her interest in us that transfixes the viewer: she does not desire us or want to know us. She does not see us; she is entirely self-regarding. I am sure that she is genuine.

'She's beautiful,' I say. 'Where did you find her?'

'She belonged to a *vieille grande dame*, a Parisian aristocrat called Gloriette de Beauville. I have a stud farm in Normandy and I visited her country house there. On the wall of her drawing room was this painting,' Cahane answers.

'May I have a look at her back?' I ask.

Cahane calls Zvi in from his other duties and he helps me lift the nude off the wall. I can smell the garlic and cigarettes on his breath as he sighs under the weight of the heavy frame. Caroline and Christopher come closer as I turn the canvas over and put it face down on a low table in the centre of the room. Esta asks if she can take Eli out into the garden to play and Cahane leads her through to the dining room and out of the French doors there, then comes back into the sitting room to join Bernstein's Anatomy Lesson.

The back of the canvas is bare, except for two small labels. The first, a rectangular brown one with a black border, is what I expect to find: it reads *ZBOROWSKI 3 rue Joseph Barra*. During the winter of 1916 to 1917, at the dead centre of the First World War raging around them, the Polish poet Leopold Zborowski moved to an apartment in the *sixième arrondissement* and offered Modigliani a space in which to live and work there. He provided him with materials and models and each month gave him about three hundred francs, in return receiving all of the works that the artist produced under his care. He continued to buy Modigliani's works until the painter's death from tuberculosis in 1920.

'It's what I thought I'd see for a work from this late period. Zborowski was a poet and Modigliani's close friend and dealer at the time. He kept him alive; at least for a while,' I say. 'He was probably a countryman of yours, Christopher,' I add.

'And of yours also, then,' Christopher replies.

'I suppose you're right. I never think of it like that.'

The second label is a beautiful eggshell blue and badly torn. It reads ICHEL HA and is one I have seen on a number of other French paintings – a Picasso, a Vlaminck and a Derain – from the first two decades of the twentieth century. The Jewish collector from Alsace-Lorraine, Michel Haas, must have bought the nude from Zborowski, probably within eighteen months of it being painted. He had a magnificent townhouse on the Île de la Cité, which the Nazis confiscated when they marched into Paris. Haas himself was sent with his wife and young son to the camp at Drancy and then to Auschwitz. Perhaps he even stood in line for soup with Fishel and Isy there.

Haas was always a buyer and a seller of pictures. Some he kept right up to the moment that his home and all of its contents were swallowed up into the gaping mouth of history. Others he sold when his income from the coalmines that he owned in his home region waned; still others he exchanged for newer, more daring masterpieces by the French and European *avant-garde*. At one time he owned three canvases by Modigliani. Perhaps the redhead had flown the nest before the Nazis marched onto the scene. I can see no obvious sign of its having been looted. I am just about to ask Zvi to help me hang the painting on the wall again when I notice something almost hidden beneath the inside edge of the back of the stretcher. I gently push against the canvas and see a small, round black stamp impregnated into its finely woven surface. It is an eagle clutching a swastika in its razor-sharp claws.

'Well, I can tell you that she left Zborowski for the well-known Jewish collector, Michel Haas,' I say. 'And that her separation from Haas wasn't an amicable one.'

'What are you saying?' Cahane asks sharply, all of the *bonhomie* and hollow charm gone from his voice.

'I'm saying that the nude probably left Monsieur Haas under duress, Mr Cahane. From my past research, I know that the National Socialists appropriated all of his possessions when they occupied his Paris home after he was deported. Even though the official line was that modern artists were "degenerate" – no one more so, perhaps, than the Jew Amedeo Modigliani – it can't have stopped some official or other from taking the painting; hanging it on his wall or selling it through a collaborationist dealer. I am also saying that Haas's relatives or descendants are probably still alive, unaware that this nude used to belong to him and was stolen.'

'I bought the painting legitimately, Mr Bernstein. I paid de Beauville thirty million francs in cash for it,' Cahane says. 'I must ask you to leave.'

'But you didn't ask her how her family came by it,' I reply. 'It wasn't hers to sell. It belongs to someone whom the nude now needs to find.'

'I bought it and it belongs to me,' Cahane says again. 'Zvi will show you out.'

'Mr Cahane, I'll tell Julius Neuberger how beautiful the nude is, but I'll also have to inform the Commission for Looted Art in London about my suspicions,' I reply.

'You can tell them what you like; the nude won't be here when they call. I have many homes, Mr Bernstein.'

'We have just the one,' Caroline suddenly says. 'No guest who has ever come there has been treated so rudely as here. You have not even offered Mr Street a glass of water. He is an old man and not used to the climate here.'

'There are several cafés in Safed,' is all that Cahane replies.

After Zvi has gone into the garden to tell Esta that the guests are leaving, he ushers us or, more precisely, muscles us to the door, blocking the corridor behind us and pushing us with his presence. We emerge out into the daylight of Safed again and Caroline says, 'Well, he was nice, wasn't he?'

'Yes, a real charmer,' I reply. 'I am sure that the Modigliani was right, though. It's a real pity; Julius would love it. It's rather ironic that Cahane, a Jew, is so unconcerned about war loot. You'd have thought the bastard would be a little more understanding.'

'He's a businessman, Charley. He's not used to doing deals that he may lose. What would happen if the Commission for Looted Art found out where the Modigliani was?'

'Oh, all they can really do is try to trace Haas's descendants and let them know that they have located a work that once belonged to him. Knowing how the story often goes, the descendants would get hold of a very good lawyer: let's face it, war loot is big business these days. Many current owners – museums, galleries or private collectors – feel compelled to reach a settlement with the heirs, even though the law itself is a little grey. Often the work in question is put for auction and the current owner and the heirs split the proceeds fifty-fifty.'

'Well, that won't happen if Cahane can help it, I imagine,' Caroline replies.

'No, he wouldn't like an even split,' I say.

'He told me on the telephone that he had been twice married and twice divorced,' Esta adds. 'His *poor* ex-wives.'

'Literally, I am sure,' Caroline says with a laugh.

Christopher has been silent for most of the morning, only saying one or two words when we met Cahane and hardly anything since. While we are drinking coffee in a small coffeehouse beside one of Safed's oldest synagogues where we are the only guests, Esta, Eli and Caroline sitting at one cramped table and me and Christopher at another, I ask him why he is so quiet.

'It is what Mr Rotstein told us about the camps. It goes round and round in my mind,' he replies. 'I cannot get it to leave; it is almost as if I myself were there.'

'What he told us of those times was very powerful; I am not surprised that you have difficulty forgetting,' I say.

'It is not like that,' Christopher answers. 'It is not that I cannot forget; it is as if I am remembering. I don't know what, Tcharley. His words seemed to tell me something I already knew.'

'You said that you'd seen images from the camps on television in New York. Perhaps what you're remembering is echoes of the footage that you saw.'

'Perhaps. I don't know. My mind is confused and does not know what it knows or what it has seen,' he says.

For our last evening in Israel, Esta prepares a meal in Christopher's honour. Eli is asleep in his bedroom and we sit at the small table in the dining room of her apartment, drinking a white wine like retsina and eating the delicate fish that she has prepared. Through the window, I can see the sun setting over the ocean, its red-orange light diffused by the haze. A large passenger plane comes in to land at the airport and the roof shudders as it passes overhead.

'What are you going to do about the Modigliani, Charley?' Esta asks.

'I think that ultimately I'll have to let Julius figure that out,' I reply. 'He's the one who wants to own it and he'll have to decide whether to report it or not. I'll tell him categorically that if he has any damned scruples he *should* do so. I'm just so happy to have seen the nude's beauty but it's not something I covet. I've never really been interested in *owning* things as such, more in looking at them from a safe distance. Ownership always implies so much responsibility.'

'In that particular case, it also implies a hell of a lot of money,' Caroline says with a laugh. 'More to the point, Charley, what are you going to do with what Fishel told us the other day?' she adds.

'Well, that's a cause I will definitely fight for. I really believe that his story deserves telling. Christopher found it particularly moving, didn't you, Christopher?'

'What he told me – us – about his memories was so powerful that it made me feel that I had a past. A past that is still somewhere out there in the world or somewhere inside of me. I just need to find it somehow, whatever time I have left and whatever it tells me about myself.'

'We'll drink to that,' Esta says. '*L'Chaim*,' she adds as we all clink glasses.

The weather has turned cold the next morning and the sky is as grey and dull as unpolished steel. Esta drives us to the airport for the afternoon flight to Heathrow and we are all silent in the Jeep as we leave the city behind us, driving north along the busy road.

After we have said our goodbyes to Esta and are about to go through customs, we turn to wave one last time. She is holding Eli in her arms and takes his hand gently in her own, teaching him how to wave back to us. Christopher blows him a puckered kiss and then turns away, walking with Caroline towards the departure lounge. He misses the smile that I see light up Eli's face; a smile that the young child will have forgotten by tomorrow.

26

Thursday, 24th December 1942

Our little Eva writes the following to her mother in a letter that has been passed on to me through the Red Cross, I fear because Miriam is now lost: 'Dearest Mummy, I hope that you are well. I am healthy and visiting aunty Frieda. I send you all many kisses. Your Eva.' The letter is dated the 8th September 1942. If only her mother could see this letter: she would be so happy. Sadly this cannot be so.

Thursday, 14th January 1943

General Winter has presented himself for service again in the New Year: we recorded twenty degrees below once, although today it has become milder again.

Friday, 15th January 1943

The following news from the field of battle was announced yesterday in a Wehrmacht *report:* 'The Supreme Command of the Wehrmacht *announces that, after the heavy losses it suffered yesterday, the enemy led only isolated and disconnected attacks in the western Caucasus, which were repelled ... Between the Caucasus and the Don and its environs, Soviet attacks failed and they suffered the loss of twenty-six armoured vehicles ... Near Stalingrad German troops heroically repulsed fierce infantry and tank attacks in heavy battles ... The* Luftwaffe *joined in at the fiercest points of battle on the earth below ... In Libya, German and Italian fighter pilots, suffering two German losses to artillery flack, took out three enemy planes ... In Tunisia, repeated offensives by enemy powers were resisted ... During daytime attacks by British plane formations on the occupied western territories, five enemy planes were shot down – in the North Sea area two... In the late evening hours, British planes attacked the western part of Germany, particularly the town of Essen. The population suffered losses. There was widespread damage to buildings ... During daylight hours, German planes attacked installations on the South Coast of England, during the night the town and the shipyards of Sunderland. Extensive fires were observed ...'*

Monday, 1st February 1943

For some weeks now I have been accompanying our people to the place of work at five o'clock in the morning, then coming back alone. The way home is mostly more interesting than the way there, as I meet Jews, Ukrainians, Poles; French and Russian prisoners-of-war, sometimes even Dutch people. I often think about the fact that today all people around the globe are directly or indirectly working for the war. A race to destruction is taking place on our earth.

Monday, 8th March 1943, midday

No diary entries for more than one month now, although in February so much happened, particularly on the field of battle. For days the weather has been more beautiful, more spring-like. By midday you can feel the sun's rays doing you good, although at night, as well as in the evening and the morning, it is still quite cold.

Often, all too often, we are reminded of our tragic fate. The times for us are very disturbed and our future is dark. It seems that we represent a kind of misfortune, or else we are particularly unlucky bearers of an unhappy existence.

Saturday, 13th March 1943, six o'clock in the morning

For the whole winter I have gone with our people as far as the place of work each morning. It takes one hour there and back and it is a beautiful walk through a pine forest. Today I heard for the first time this year a songbird warbling its song; I am not clear if it was a thrush or not.

Almost every day when it is still dark I come across a man, roughly my height, who whistles out his little songs powerfully and in a carefree manner. I have often thought about how he could be so disposed to whistle his songs out into the world every day at so early an hour. The mornings are now already bright and today he came up to me and asked me for a light in a foreign language. As I was searching for one, he offered me a cigarette as well, but I could not give him a light as I could not find one on me. He excused himself, as I did, and it dawned on me that he was a Dutch munitions worker who used to live with us, like many others, in the camp. No longer will we now stroll silently past each other, but will exchange greetings instead.

Friday, 30th April 1943

. . .

After some three months I have received a greetings card from Miriam. It was sent on the 27th, the same day that I wrote and sent a birthday letter to her. We were united in our thoughts and our letters crossed paths.

Thursday, 27th May 1943

The most beautiful month of the year is now almost over. The whole month was warm and sunny. I only had the pleasure of going bathing once, as bathing is forbidden to us. Bathing is only allowed for the Germans, the Belgians, the French and workers from the east.

The theatre of war is quiet at the moment. No major action is being reported from the east. The war in Africa has been over for more than a week. The German and Italian troops had to cease their fight there due to a lack of reinforcements. The British and American forces had a superior power of ten to one against the Axis troops.

Wednesday, 2nd June 1943

I am very keen to know how my friends are after the terrible bombardment of my beloved hometown, Wuppertal-Elberfeld. I have read about the bombing raids in the Wehrmacht *reports of 31st May. I was born there and lived there for twenty years: I know every corner of the town and much of it has now been destroyed. If only I had news from my friends.*

Tuesday, 15th June 1943

I am shaken to the core, having read the following sentence in the paper: 'Whoever thinks that they have a valid complaint about this or that unavoidable collateral damage of war should take a look at Essen, Dortmund, Bochum, Wuppertal, or the other towns affected by the aerial bombardment and blush with shame that he dares to compare his troubles and hardships caused by the war to the sufferings of the populations of those towns.' Does not this sentence hold a terrible, sober truth about unspeakable suffering? Of the many aerial bombardments, Wuppertal is named in fourth place. That says all that needs to be said.

Saturday, 26th June 1943

Yesterday was a fateful day for me. After long days of unconscious existence, I was suddenly confronted with myself. I saw it and could have seen it long before if I had only looked into myself more often and more closely: now that it is almost too late I can clearly see a character flaw within me and will try to change it.

There has been another terrible air raid on Wuppertal-Elberfeld. The population has suffered heavy losses. I am receiving no news from my loved ones, yet my letters are also not being returned to me. What can one do but wait? Great miracles take place every day, if one thinks of the civilian population and the heroism of its suffering. The unknown path that we follow is one of suffering and change. The dead go before us and show us the way.

27

Winter has England in its clenched white grip. An early snow shrouds the countryside as the train takes us from King's Cross northwards out through the flat expanses of Hertfordshire and Cambridgeshire. Here and there, the light from the carriage windows picks out the dark forms of rabbits frozen still on the edges of fields.

Cambridge in early November is bitterly cold; it is dark by six. The first thing that Christopher says when we pull up outside the house in the taxi from the station is that he imagined it standing alone in its own grounds, not as part of a terrace.

'They say that an Englishman's home is his castle, Christopher,' Caroline laughs, 'even if the Englishman in this case is me – I was left the house by an aunt – and it isn't really much of a castle, more of a worker's two-up-two-down. In this city even this little house would cost an awful lot of money.'

'It already feels like home because it belongs to you,' Christopher says with a gentle smile.

Once we have shown Christopher his small bedroom, with its single bed, wooden clothes rail and white-tiled shower cubicle behind a white door, Caroline prepares a meal of potato salad and grilled lamb chops while I light the fire. Christopher sits in an armchair as the flames catch a slow hold of the damp logs that whistle and steam in the grate.

'You're like the grandfather I never had,' I joke. 'We should find you a pipe.'

'Perhaps one of those ones like the Bedouin men were smoking,' he replies, looking into the fire with our black cat on his lap.

The next morning I have to return to Conduit Street. London is like an ant's nest: workers march in lines along the streets to sit at Formica desks, following a logic that I can only guess at. I have not been to my room for more than two weeks, but little has changed in my absence. The red Cyclops-eye of my answer phone blinks at me and there are a handful of letters. Most are bills or invoices, with only one hand-written note of thanks from a local Mayfair gallery-owner whom I helped with unravelling the provenance of an early Dutch-period van Gogh.

The message is from Julius. The tape slurs his speech, making him drawl like a Southerner. 'Hi, Charley,' he says. 'Just wanned to checkout howya godawn in Isreel. Guess yar not back'll try lader.'

I need to tell him about our visit to Cahane and his illegitimate nude, but decide to wait until I get back to Cambridge. I am not ready to get down to work again quite yet. I leave my room and walk up to Oxford Circus Underground station, taking the Victoria Line three stops north to King's Cross. Instead of entering the bustle and throng of the mainline concourse, I take the two sets of escalators up from the depths of the Victoria Line and walk down the short stairs to the Circle Line, as if these two Tube tracks existed in an Escher-like universe that does not connect up logically but blinds us with its *trompe l'œil*.

The Circle Line train takes nine minutes to arrive. A stray pigeon has penetrated into the labyrinth of tunnels and hobbles on its deformed pink feet, gnarled like the hands of sufferers of wet leprosy, across the terrain of cigarette butts, drifting sweet-wrappers and abstract blots and blights of chewing gum.

The train, almost as crippled as the bird, limps eastwards station-by-station to Liverpool Street. I get off and walk further east, hoping that my spontaneous decision to visit Deborah in her studio will be met by her presence there.

As there is no reply from her door on Fournier Street, I walk round to the back of the building to see if I can look into the large windows of her studio. They are shut but not curtained or closed off to the world with blinds; windows allowing in the objective scrutiny of light, even when the easel holds a less-than-true masterpiece by Deborah's own hand.

I am lost in a world of fragmented thoughts and do not notice a pair of blue-green eyes staring at me with amusement through the reflective glass that directs the weak sunlight straight into my face. A muffled, 'Charley, what are you doing out there with the bins?' pinpoints Deborah for me. I gesticulate that I will go back round to the front door again.

Once she has let me into her studio with a kiss on each cheek, holding both of her arms out with a cigarette in one hand and a cup of black coffee in the other, I say 'Where did you appear from?'

'I was here all along, I just wasn't answering the door. Thought you might be the Inland Revenue.'

'I'd better not ask,' I reply.

'So, how was it? Did my protégé get through without any problems?'

'Without a hitch. As far as the authorities were concerned, he was my long-lost grandfather, Lebrecht, for the entire trip. It kind of suited him; now he's back to being his old self again: nameless and rootless. I wish I knew how to help him more than I am. I just don't know what else I can do now: nothing seems to do any good and I can tell he's becoming more and more depressed.'

'I suppose time's the only thing that can possibly make a difference; that or a miracle. At least he's with you and Caroline now. I'm sure that he feels at home with you both.'

'He says that he does, but I still worry that taking him out of New York was not the best move. We've given him a great Middle Eastern tour, but it's not brought him any nearer to himself as far as I can see.'

'Charley, men are fixers; they want to make the world right through practical solutions, inventions, things. Life's sometimes a bit more mystical and subtle. Trust a woman's intuition: something will happen, that's all I'm saying. Have faith.'

'The faith bit's a complex one,' I reply.

While Deborah makes me a coffee – 'No milk, it's off I'm afraid' – I look at the work in progress on her easel. This time it is a difficult restoration: an area of thick impasto on a *Nabis* landscape by Gauguin from his time in Brittany in the late 1880s has begun to flake. Like a cartographer of the heavens, Deborah is filling in the constellation of minute paint-losses in the sky with the finest of sable brushes.

'It's funny,' I say as she brings me the coffee, 'I just had an idea.'

'Another one of your practical solutions, Charley?'

'Well, an inelegant one perhaps. The Modigliani we saw in Israel was to die for, but I'm sure it's war loot and Julius won't go near it if he's got any sense.'

'Aren't the beautiful ones always the biggest trouble?' Deborah says.

'The owner gave me a transparency to show to Julius. You could copy it and sell him the reproduction for, say, twenty grand. Less than a thousandth of the owner's asking price and without the incriminating labels.'

'What about the aura of the original, Charley?'

'Yes, you're right. I'm sure Julius would never buy it.'

I am on the slow train to Cambridge from Liverpool Street again. It is mid-afternoon, before the hour when commuters pour out of the City for the suburbs and the market towns of Essex. The train is three-quarters empty; four young children run amok at the other end of the carriage, watched over by a mother in her early thirties who looks as if she has seen a very frightening ghost.

It is another cold day, but the under-seat heater blows out air that warms my feet and legs and creates a fuggy atmosphere in the carriage. The old seats are soft and, apart from the occasional squeals and shouts that the children make as they play, the carriage is quiet and I soon fall asleep.

I hardly ever remember my dreams and usually wake up not

knowing if I have dreamt at all. The syncopated rhythm of the train's wheels running over the rails must have penetrated into my sleeping mind somehow: I come to near Cambridge with Christopher's bright blue eyes staring into my mind's eye; a peaceful expression, neither a smile nor a frown, on his face. A voice, not Christopher's heavily accented timbre but a whispering childish one, repeats over and over, *It'll come for him* soon, *It'll come for him* soon, *It'll come for him* soon, *It'll come for him* soon...

The wind sends its icy fingers down my spine as I leave Cambridge station and walk the shortest route home.

Caroline has spent the day showing Christopher around the colleges in the thin layer of snow that still clings to the frozen ground. At this time of year, the city is denuded of tourists and the university is left to its own devices; townspeople go about their business and villagers come into the mediaeval system of streets from the Fens, to visit the market and the endless chains of clothing stores, cafés and restaurants.

'Tcharley, it is a beautiful city,' Christopher says once I have taken off my coat and gloves. 'I was thinking that these ancient buildings must have been skyscrapers when they were made.'

'The tallest buildings in the land were cathedrals and castles, built high up on natural or man-made hills. Ely cathedral, fifteen miles from here, stood out alone in the middle of the Fens, the dead flat land, like a hand raised up to God. Just imagine what power it must have held for people seeing it for the first time five hundred years ago. A bit like when you first saw a skyscraper rising into the clouds.'

'Less towards God than Mammon in that case,' Caroline adds.

'*Maman?*' Christopher asks uncertainly.

'It was a joke: Mammon is the ancient god of wealth,' she answers. 'Something most academics here know very little about.'

'I know the feeling,' I say. 'Talking of money, I need to speak to Julius, but want to show Christopher something first.'

I walk upstairs and take the blue velvet bag with its amber beads out from beneath some shirts and jumpers in the bottom of the chest of drawers in our bedroom. It is the first time that I have looked at them since my return from New York in the late spring; they take the warmth of my hands and their dark curvatures reflect the lamplight from the ceiling above. Like Christopher, they are mute witnesses; beautiful mysteries that appear transparent but turn every question that you ask of them blankly back on itself.

I take the beads downstairs cupped in both hands and ask Christopher to hold out his ancient hands, like a supplicant. 'These are my grandmother Miriam's beads that I told you about. You remember, my mother brought them over with her when she came here in '39,' I say. 'I'm sure there were once enough for a whole necklace, but they got lost over time. They disappeared into history one by one like the members of her family.'

'A rosary of loss,' Caroline says.

'Tcharley, they feel warm, as if they are living or made of blood.'

'Amber takes its warmth from your hands, Christopher; it feeds off your body heat as you hold them. The life-warmth that you feel comes from my hands to yours – a message,' I reply.

Christopher sits with the beads for a long time, looking at them now and then and listening to the soft clacking sounds that they make as he pours them from one hand into the other. He seems deep in thought and is very quiet as I read and Caroline works at her computer in the dining room.

At around quarter to ten, after we have eaten supper and are all sitting quietly looking into the fire, Caroline and I on the sofa and Christopher in his chair by the hearth, he hands the beads back to me and says that he is going to go up to bed; that he is very tired. We say goodnight to him and he climbs the stairs that creak even under the weight of his slight frame. I hear the water running in the bathroom and imagine him washing his face and hands in the water from the sink, as I saw him do so many times in the Manhasset Hospital, remembering how he first rubbed his face in a circular motion with the flannel and then moved his hand round to the back of his neck and behind his ears. Christopher washes himself like an animal might wash itself; following instinct, not pleasure. He had to be persuaded by Nurse Kowalski to take a bath perhaps twice a week, preferring as he did a military-style standing wash each morning and evening, never taking off his white vest top or his blue-and-white striped pyjama trousers.

Caroline and I are watching a story about a breakdown in Israeli-Arab talks on the ten o'clock news when the telephone rings. I walk into the dining room and answer it as quickly as possible, hoping that the upstairs telephone will not have disturbed Christopher. It is Julius, just about to shut the gallery for the day in New York.

'How *was* it?' he asks in a voice that booms and ebbs and flows through the ether.

'What, the trip or the nude?' I reply.

'Both of course, Charley. Betcha can guess, though, which one I'm really asking about.'

'She was incredibly beautiful: one of Modigliani's great late works in my opinion. I had never seen it in the literature before, but I'm sure it's right. The trip was pretty good as well, now that you ask: we even got as far as Egypt and Mount Sinai.'

'Moses taking the tablets and everything?'

'Something like that, yes. The trouble is, Julius, your nude has a few personality problems. She's got a troubled past.'

'What's the matter with her? Don't tell me it's anything terminal, Charley.'

'It probably is, I'm afraid: at least in terms of your relationship with her. I'm almost certain she was stolen in Paris by the Nazis during the Second World War.'

'*And?*'

'And that the heirs are somewhere out there still. You wouldn't want to buy something you might later have to return, would you?'

'How beautiful was she again, on a scale of one to ten?'

'She was a ten, Julius.'

'Then we'll have to see, we'll have to damned well see,' he repeats. 'When canya get back to the Big Apple so that we can catch up on this further?'

'I wasn't planning to go back to New York for a while. I'll have to see: I've got quite a lot to do here.'

'Well, the sooner the better: it's important. Give me a ring from your office later in the week,' he says, hanging up with a cursory goodbye.

Caroline and I are getting ready for bed, me lying in the bath and her taking off her make-up and moisturising her face and hands. 'Christopher seems so very sad at the moment,' she whispers, leaning down towards my ear. She smells like freshly cut peaches.

'When I first had the idea of bringing him with us over to Europe, I thought that taking him physically nearer to where he originally came from might help,' I say, trying to keep my voice low. 'Of course, in reality it hasn't really made any difference at all.'

'There was never going to be a magic cure,' she replies. 'He knew that as well as you and I did.'

'What do you think we do now?' I ask quietly.

'What can anyone do but wait, Charley?'

We are lying in bed in the dark, a sliver of orange light coming through the gap in the curtains from the streetlamp outside the window, when Caroline suddenly sits up in bed and says that she can hear a strange noise. 'Sounds like the cat howling in the garden or something,' she says as she gets out of bed and opens the door of our bedroom before I have time to offer to go and see what is happening. I hear her tiptoe down the stairs, then come back up after a few minutes of silence. She walks down the hall towards Christopher's room, her quiet footsteps stopping outside his door. I wait for her to come back to bed, imagining our female cat in a fight with the local ginger tom that prowls his territory at night up and down the street and through the gardens at the back of the terrace.

I must have fallen asleep. I wake up with a start, Caroline gently shaking my arm and whispering '*Charley, Charley!*' as I search for her face in the dark.

'What is it?'

'It's Christopher; he's been in a terrible state. I've just spent almost an hour in his room trying to comfort him. The noise we heard was him crying, not the cat: Christopher sobbing into his pillow almost uncontrollably. I've managed to calm him down a bit and he's going to sleep, I hope.'

'Do you want me to go and sit with him for a while?'

'No, you'd better leave him now. Let him rest and we can talk to him in the morning, in the rational light of day. He said that he'd heard you mention something about going back to New York and thought that we wanted him to go back to the hospital.'

'That's ridiculous: I can only think that he overheard part of my chat with Julius,' I reply.

'It could be that, yes. He must have come quietly down the stairs for something, perhaps a glass of water, just when you mentioned New York to Julius. Then gone back up straight away without us hearing, taking it all out of context.'

'Anyway, what does he think now? Admittedly, he can't stay here forever, but we are going to try and work something out for him and not bloody well abandon him back there.'

'Charley, he knows that. Let's go to sleep, it's very late,' she says as she puts her head on my chest.

I am wide-awake with worry and tell myself to try to calm down as I stroke her soft hair, as much to soothe myself as to send her to sleep. After a few minutes, Caroline's breathing becomes softer and slower. I listen to the tides of her sleep as I lie with the weight of her head above my beating heart, imagining its anxious rhythms entering her dream world; the rattling sound of a slow goods train over old tracks sixty years ago, hands visible between the slatted wooden walls. I look through the slit in the curtain at the seeping orange light. This journey's destination frightens me sometimes; it really frightens me.

28

The next morning we wake up late; the house is bathed in light and silence. Christopher is fully dressed when we go downstairs, sitting in his favourite chair and drinking a cup of tea with a slice of lemon floating in it like the sun's reflection on water.

We eat breakfast at the dining table in near silence; I am tired after a night of restless sleep and Caroline seems subdued. 'How are you this morning, Christopher?' she asks quietly. 'Do you feel better today?'

'Tcharley, Caroline, I am very sorry – embarrassed I mean – about last night. It will not happen again. You have both been very good to me, more than I can say. Sometimes this emptiness gets inside me, that is all. I must stop it from hurting me.'

'When you feel unhappy you must talk to us about it,' I reply. 'We are always here to listen.'

'I am not as good at talking as you both are,' he replies.

After breakfast, Caroline says that she will drive us out to Ely for a walk around the cathedral. The weather is still bitterly cold but the sky is beautiful and bright, burnished by the pale winter sun. Long before we enter the small city, we can see the cathedral rising dark against the horizon as if it is floating above the Fen landscape.

As we arrive, members of the congregation are filtering out of the low wooden entrance that is let into the mighty oak diptych of doors with their iron flanges and studs. Inside, hushed voices and echoing footsteps rise up to the great vaulted ceiling. While Caroline and I walk down the aisle to the right of the nave, I watch Christopher moving down the nave itself between the rows of wooden pews, separated from us by the stride of great Norman arches that repeat themselves, ever smaller in scale like a fading echo or a ripple, up towards the roof. We meet at the area called the lantern, just before the choir, and look up at the light coming through the stained-glass windows. As we talk, a cloud must have been swept by the wind from in front of the sun: a shaft of light, pale blue and pink from the windows, falls across Christopher's face like a benediction.

'Look, the light's given you a blessing,' Caroline says.

'It's blinding me,' he replies. 'I cannot see what the windows show.'

'Talk about coincidences: that one's of St Christopher carrying the Christ Child across the water, as far as I can make out from down here,' I answer, pointing up to a vivid blue and red window showing a bearded man carrying an infant in his arms. 'The child Christians call the Son of God was carried to safety by a man with your name.'

'It is not my name,' he says. 'Just as you called me Lebrecht to get me out of New York, other people gave me the name Christopher. It is not what I call myself, Tcharley.'

'What do you call yourself, then?' Caroline says softly.

'*Der Pechvogel*. This is how I address myself in my thoughts.'

'What does that mean? It's German, isn't it?' she asks.

'Yes, it is,' I reply. 'It means the bearer of bad luck; an ill omen.'

'I know now for sure that I will never find out who I am,' Christopher says.

'How can you be so certain? Please give it time, Christopher, please be patient. It has only been one year,' I reply, but he is not listening: he has turned away and begun to walk back up the nave towards the door.

In the afternoon once we have returned from Ely, we leave Christopher at home in front of the fire with the promise that we will be back before five o'clock. Caroline cycles into town to her faculty to mark some undergraduate essays and I walk the mile into the centre to the marketplace.

It is already past three and some of the stallholders – the flower-sellers, the cheese-merchants, the man who sells second-rate second-hand books – are already clearing up and closing for the day. I buy Caroline two bunches of white and purple irises and walk around the market looking for something as a present for Christopher. Most of the stalls are selling food; I buy some fruit and vegetables and three rainbow trout for supper. At a bric-a-brac stall I look through the assorted odds and ends, marble rolling pins, old blue and white enamel tins for flour and biscuits, broken weighing-scales, but what catches my eye is an antique kaleidoscope. I look into it, turning it hand against hand, as if into a telescope held up to view some distant nebula or galaxy. The fragments of colour fall towards themselves over and over, round and round, hypnotising me.

'It's a nice 'un, isn't it?' the man behind the stall says suddenly. 'It's Victorian.'

'Yes, it is. How much are you asking for it?'

'Seeing as it's a weekday 'n' all and if it's fer yer kid, we'll say thirty.'

'Well, let's say it's for an old man who's young at heart,' I reply. 'He needs some cheering up. Can you do it for twenty-five?'

'Okay, it's a deal,' he says.

On the way back to the house, I walk to Caroline's faculty of ancient history. The main door is locked and I ring the bell; after five minutes she comes down with a thick file of papers and says that she wants to get a coffee on the way home. We walk down towards Mill Road to a café and sit drinking coffee and talking about her students' essays and what we should do for Christmas and New Year.

'I think we should go somewhere exotic, like Zanzibar,' she says.

'What about Christopher?'

'We can take him with us; we haven't got any children yet. It'll be good practice, Charley.'

'Well, let's see how the next couple of weeks go and whether I can get enough work to make some money.'

We walk home through the graveyard off Mill Road, the grass around the gravestones freshly cut but the stones themselves overgrown or knocked awry by time and vandals. It is already getting dark and Caroline holds my arm tightly as we walk through the pitch-black avenue of beeches and conifers that leads to the cemetery gates. Once we have left this silent nursery of the dead, the house is a short walk away through the side streets. We get home just after a quarter-past five and find the downstairs rooms silent; the fire now reduced to embers glowing a dull red. Christopher's chair is empty.

'Christopher, we're home,' Caroline calls out.

Silence. 'Christopher,' I repeat, 'would you like a cup of tea?' There is no sound, only our cat as it rattles through the cat-flap looking for its supper.

I go upstairs to his room, but he is not there. The bed is neatly made and his few possessions – a comb, his razor, a piece of uncut lapis lazuli that Esta gave him, the book on memory that he was given in New York – are laid out on his bedside table. A tap drips in the bathroom, but it is also empty. The curtains in our bedroom flap and flutter in the winter wind coming through the open window.

'He must have gone out for a walk,' Caroline says when I come downstairs again.

'I might be gone for some time,' I joke stupidly, nervous with not knowing what to do. 'Do you think we should call the police?'

'Don't be so silly, Charley. What do you think they would say to us?'

'That we should wait for him here?'

'Precisely.'

'It's not like him to disappear, though,' I say.

We grill the trout and prepare the vegetables for supper, leaving Christopher's to be reheated in the oven when he returns. Caroline and I eat in silence, listening out for any slight sound that might betray his presence. The fish and vegetables are delicious, but I feel guilty even thinking about enjoying my food in this atmosphere of quietly but palpably growing anxiety and alarm.

'Where on earth *is* he?' Caroline says to break the silence. It is now almost half-past seven. I reach to switch on the television to distract myself, but she says that we should keep it off – or at least watch it on mute – so that we can listen out for Christopher.

At just past eight o'clock, I go upstairs to the bathroom. I am sure that something must be wrong, but do not want to upset Caroline or shape this fear into words and therefore make it real, alive. I walk back along the dark corridor towards the top of the stairs and see something that I did not notice earlier: a halo of light coming through the frame of the wooden hatch to the attic outside our bedroom.

I pull the cord that brings the retractable ladder down from its slot in the attic above and climb up, pushing the hatch upwards as my head reaches the height of the corridor's ceiling. The bare bulb is burning brightly as I emerge head and shoulders into the attic, and it casts a harsh light on the most terrible thing that I have ever seen.

Christopher is half standing, half kneeling at the back of the attic nearest the garden. He must have come up here, pulling the ladder back up – I remember thinking – and closing the hatch behind him. There is a length of white electrical flex around his neck, tied to one of the sloping beams that make up the roof. His eyes are staring out blankly from his head and his lips are blue, parted by a swollen purple tongue. A scream catches in my throat. I try again and again but cannot speak, hearing only a disembodied groaning noise coming from some place behind me; the sound that a wounded animal might make. It is only later that I realise that this unutterable sound was coming from me. The scream emerges as I hold Christopher and undo the noose around his neck; now the scream will not stop. I hear the sound of feet running up the stairs and Caroline's concerned voice behind me, then her shrieks mingling with my own.

She must have called an ambulance: I hear its siren outside the front of the house and suddenly two paramedics are either side of Christopher, who is laid along the wide plank walkway that runs the length of the attic. They give him heart massage and mouth-to-mouth resuscitation for what seems like an eternity. By the end, they are breathing hard and saying that it is no good; he is lost.

The paramedics fetch a stretcher and strap Christopher into it, then manoeuvre him awkwardly down the ladder and into his bedroom. The last time he was in this room he was alive, I keep thinking. He went up the ladder a living being and came down dead. *Dead dead dead dead DEAD*, Julian's voice keeps saying, over and over. It will not stop. It will not stop.

I am having an out-of-body experience; this is all happening to someone else. The police arrive and ask me questions and then talk to Caroline as she drinks tea laden with spoonfuls of sugar against the shock. She keeps crying and crying and cannot seem to stop. The policemen are young men: the older one must be only thirty – younger than me – and the other one barely twenty-five. They are obviously embarrassed by our distress and take down cursory details – 'Name?' 'Lebrecht Rittershaus.' 'Relationship?' 'My grandfather.' – as the paramedics shut the front door quietly behind them and drive off with the siren silenced. There is no urgency any more: *We have all the time in the world*, they seem to be saying. *We have all the time in the world* ... Time seems to have stopped.

The policemen are kind: having notified the coroner, they arrange for the body to be taken to the hospital morgue later in the evening, so that we have time to sit with Christopher and prepare him for his journey to the cold touch of the post-mortem table. 'It's up to the coroner to make the formal verdict; there'll have to be an inquest, but it seems like a straightforward suicide. We're very sorry, madam; we're very sorry, sir. Our condolences,' they say in unison as they go.

Caroline's eyes are puffy and red and I guess mine are too as we work, washing Christopher's head and neck, as if to soothe his face contorted into a lopsided grin by rigor mortis and to wipe away the marks made by the noose, and bathe his hands and feet with warm water – 'It *must* be warm, Charley,' she says between sobs, 'even if he can't feel it.' She holds him while I take off his thin jumper with its patch of dried saliva and his soiled blue cotton trousers, so that we can lay him out in something better than this. He is so thin, just skin and bone: a rag-and-bone man. I realise that this is the first time I have ever seen his upper body naked: even when he washed himself at the sink in the Manhasset Hospital he always wore a vest. There is a dark wine-red birthmark shaped like a crescent moon under his left shoulder blade as I turn him on his side so that Caroline can wash his back.

'They say birthmarks are wounds from a past life,' Caroline says in a choked voice, running her finger around its irregular contours.

'We should never have left him on his own. He needed us, Caroline,' I reply.

'He always had us there for him; he knew that. We could not watch over him twenty-four hours a day.'

The undertakers do not arrive until almost half-past eleven. Most of the lights along our street are out as if the houses are in mourning. There are two undertakers in dark suits, carrying black leather cases like medical bags: doctors for the dead. They go upstairs and we sit and wait downstairs on the sofa, Caroline wrapped in a blanket and me still feeling that all of this is happening to someone else. I am almost smiling with the shock of it all. It is amazing how much your hands can shake when they want to.

At one point as the men are bringing the black body bag down the stairs, we hear a loud thud as they slip and Christopher's head catches a step. Caroline shudders and flinches beside me involuntarily, as if his dead body could still feel pain. The bag seems to be only half-filled by his birdlike corpse as they load it into the back of their long black car.

We finally go up to bed after two o'clock. As Caroline washes in the bathroom, I sit down on Christopher's empty bed. The kaleidoscope waits on his bedside table, looked into only by the night. I trace the compression that his head has left on the single pillow; it is cold to the touch, like stone.

I am just about to go to bed and try to get some sleep beside Caroline when I notice something white beneath a corner of the pillow. It is a folded sheet of paper, blank on the front and back but holding two lines of Christopher's spidery handwriting inside itself when I open it up, like the solution to a riddle or the good-luck charm inside a Chinese cracker. *I do not want to go back to New York. I do not want to be alone with myself any more. Forgive me*, his words say.

29

Monday, 5th July 1943

At last I have received a letter dated 23rd June from Wuppertal: my friends write that they have survived the horrors. Yet one or two days after this letter there was another attack on Wuppertal and I am worried again and long to know that they are alive.

Sunday, 18th July 1943

I have received a detailed letter from my dear friends in Wuppertal: at long last another sign of life. A localised 'end of the world', to capture it in one phrase, seems to have taken place in our beloved hometown, according to the description in the letter. It is strange: their words cannot express the horror, yet I believe that I can see everything that took place there. Many friends lost their lives.

When I read and hear these things again and again, I think back to that sentence I read about the aerial bombardment of Wuppertal. Can there be greater catastrophes than a town such as ours laid to almost complete ruin in forty minutes? What does this terrible tragedy try to shout and cry out to us, but 'Change your minds'?

Yesterday was another particularly stormy day for me: I received the thunder and lightning of that letter and then the news that we are shortly to be sent away from here.

On Sicily, German and Italian troops are fighting British and American landing forces. On the Eastern Front, an offensive has been taking place for several days.

Wednesday, 28th July 1943

The rumour that we are to leave Sternberg has sunk into the sea of silence again, yet eighty easterners have been sent away from here.

On the 27th the following announcement was made in the newspaper: 'Mussolini stepped down as leader/Change of government in Italy/Marshal Badoglio named as successor/ Appeal to the Italian people by the King.'

Saturday, 7th August 1943

For one week now the hottest weather possible: thirty or thirty-five degrees Celsius in the shade.

The war in Italy is going on as before. The British and American governments have demanded that Italy must surrender unconditionally if she wants peace. Naturally for Italy this is out of the question. On Sicily the fronts have hardly changed for more than a week.

In the east, chiefly around Orel and Bielgorod, the greatest material destruction seen so far is taking place. Thousands of battery units and tanks face each other there across the closest possible divide. The Russians attack German positions again and again with the greatest effort, but collapse bloodied when faced with the defensive power of the German troops. In the last month the Russians have lost almost eight thousand tanks and a great number of aeroplanes. Hamburg has been heavily bombed.

Early on Monday an appeal was made to the population of Berlin to leave the city if at all possible so as to minimise the victims of any aerial bombardments.

Thursday, 19th August 1943

The fighting on Sicily, which began on 10th July, came to an end on 17th August with the taking of the island by the Anglo-American troops. It was the heaviest possible of battles.

Thursday, 26th August 1943, 4.30 in the morning

Today the watchman woke me up with the painful news: 'It is the last time that I will wake you.' Yes, it has now become true that we are going away from here.

We are hearing that the other camps are also to be liquidated. We are going, now that the turn has come to us, towards a dark future, yet I am thankful to my fate that I could spend the time in this camp. We were together with French, Belgian, Dutch, Flemish, Polish, Ukrainian and Russian prisoners. I got to know a man, Fishel Rotstein, with whom, I believe, I will remain bound together through fate.

It must always get darker before it can get light again ...

30

With these words Isy's diary ends and his journey to Auschwitz began. His time there did not finish him, although the diet of bread made from flour and sawdust, the thin soup and the two bitterly cold winters that followed left him with the asthma that would eventually kill him in Melbourne many years later. He sewed the inmates' striped uniforms to survive in Auschwitz, but did not have the moral burden of commanding his fellow prisoners and reporting to the *Kommandant* that he had suffered in Sternberg, which would have meant a slow death of the conscience.

You know the story of Isy and Fishel, but it is also in some ways an unfamiliar one: the story of two men from amongst the thousands who survived Auschwitz rather than the millions who did not. For Isy and Fishel, it got light again. For my great-aunt Hedwig and for my grandmother Miriam, it got blacker and blacker, but you know that already as well. The precise how and the precise when of their deaths no one will ever know for certain. The where: Hedwig in Auschwitz and Miriam in Treblinka, those glamorous names that top the league tables of all the Third Reich's many death machines.

Because Christopher's death was sudden and unexpected, because it was not the result of natural causes and because he died alone with no one to witness what took place, the coroner for South and West Cambridgeshire must hold an inquest. The two policemen who took statements from us after we found Christopher's body come back to the house in late November with the coroner's officer to pin down the facts; to hone their understanding of the details.

Caroline and I give them Christopher's passport, telling them that my grandfather, Lebrecht, had lived alone in Germany since his wife's death in the late 1970s and that he had no other family; that my mother, his only child, was now also dead. We tell them that he would have wanted us to arrange his funeral, as we were his last remaining family; that there would be no one in Germany who would notice that he had gone. No one to miss him. We tell them that Lebrecht was beginning to betray signs that his legendary memory, the stuff of family folklore, was growing tired; that he had gone to New York shortly before his death to visit a friend, when he must have known that this friend had been dead for more than thirty years. We felt that it was our duty to go and bring him home, taking him first on a short holiday to Israel. A proud man, it must have been the gradual erosion of his faculties that had brought him to take his own life.

On the morning of the coroner's inquest, a dull day with a strong breeze rattling the skeletons of the trees, the two paramedics and policemen are present as witnesses to the facts of the case. The paramedics describe to the coroner what they found in the attic and the two policemen make their statements. We are not required to say anything, apart from confirming who we are and my relationship to the deceased.

It is, as the coroner says in his summing-up as Caroline and I sit on our hard chairs in this austere room, an open-and-shut case. He says that the post-mortem found nothing to indicate that Lebrecht Rittershaus had not died by his own hands, the noose of electrical flex impeding the flow of blood to his brain and air to his lungs; not a sudden death but a slow asphyxiation over perhaps as much as half an hour. Caroline and I hold hands ever more tightly as the images of

Christopher's gaping eyes and crooked body in the attic haunt the coroner's bald words. The coroner closes with his verdict of suicide and says that he will have to notify the German authorities of his verdict once he has released the body to us for the funeral.

Caroline and I have decided to spend Christmas at home in Cambridge; it has been nearly six weeks since Christopher's death, but he has left no dark presence behind him. He is clean gone, as Julius might say. Our house is at peace with itself, even if its occupants still move around it like sleepwalkers not knowing what to do with themselves or with their grief. The funeral was a quiet affair; Caroline, Deborah and I were the only mourners and the priest officiating at the crematorium was young and stumbled over his few words about the dearly departed and his long and rich life. Shaving nicks bloodied the collar of his crisp white shirt.

Christopher will not be back. We could not bury him because we would not have known what to put on the gravestone. It would have all been lies.

I walked with Caroline out towards Grantchester with Christopher's ashes inside a plastic urn in a rucksack on my back, stopping at a quiet bend in the River Cam called Byron's Pool. The branches of the willows and the alder bend low over the deep green river here, brushing its surface and creating eddies and swirls in the quiet current. Lord Byron, whilst a student at Cambridge in the early years of the nineteenth century, is said to have swum here. His close friend, Shelley, died by water, but that was elsewhere and later.

Caroline and I set the urn on the riverbank between us, our trousers rolled up and our feet dangling in the freezing water, and threw handfuls of the white-grey ash into the river, watching the ash-pools float slowly downstream. The birds kept up their singing, the sun shone coldly through the trees; everything stayed exactly the same, went on living. Only Christopher floated away from us, particle by particle, atom by atom: a dissolving memory.

Christmas and New Year are deathly quiet. The neighbours on both sides are away and no one has come to visit; perhaps no one wants to sleep in Christopher's bed. The thin snow is back, but it is not a white Christmas, as the light covering does not mask the greys of concrete, the blacks of tarmac and the browns of the earth. It is a *grisaille* of a winter.

Caroline and I spend the Christmas week feeding logs into the fire, walking around the deserted streets, swapping little presents and talking late into the night, half-drunk on hot punch and whisky toddies against the cold.

'Almost as good as being on the Indian Ocean,' she says with a wry laugh. 'You can't beat the freezing winds of Cambridge for an all-over tan.'

'We'll go away at Christmas next year; hopefully we'll have a bit more money by then,' I reply. 'Although it's sad here, I think that it would've felt like some kind of abandonment if we'd gone away just now.'

'I suppose you're right,' she says. 'Still, I don't think he would've wanted us to sit around and mope.'

'We're not, though, are we? After so much travelling and movement this year, it's quite nice just to *be* somewhere for a while,' I reply.

We spend New Year's Eve watching the fireworks on Midsummer Common. A large crowd of spectators has gathered on the open ground and under the dark trees that line the river. We are all wrapped in thick coats, scarves and woollen hats against the biting cold, some children even carried out by their parents from their beds and held in their arms in child-sized sleeping bags to watch the display. As midnight approaches, the disjointed voice of the crowd coalesces from a thousand separate conversations into one monologue: 'Ten, nine, eight, seven, six, five, four, three, two, OOO-NNE!' and then the endless raucous squeals of kalamazoos, car horns, a stray bagpipe, and the open throats of the crowd as we look up at the multicoloured constellations and starbursts of the fireworks raining down on us like flak or tracer fire. What a year. I cannot decide if all of this is the celebration of something now over or something about to begin. Whichever, Caroline and I hold each other tight and share a hipflask of whisky under a blanket and promise to make this new year a better one than the last.

I do not go back to Conduit Street until the second week of January. Much of the art world is still on its extended winter holiday and the tourists are kept off the streets by the weather. My room is ice-cold and I do not want to stay long, but there is one handwritten letter that keeps me in my chair. It is from Fishel.

Haifa
29th December

Dear Charley,
Since we met I have been trying as hard as I can to look back at that terrible time when I walked across the frozen land, seeing scarcely any other living soul, with the young Nazi guard as my only human contact. I have been thinking of him since your visit opened up my memories.
I believe that his fear and loyalty helped save my life, made me carry on walking and not give up and die in the snow when Isy was gone, as if taken by God from my side. I keep asking myself to remember the guard's name, or anything about him that might make him more real for you. All I can recall is his young courage, his honest face and that, one night, we found the safety of a hay-barn and slept under the cover of a roof for once in those terrible freezing days. We held each other to keep warm, me lying with my chest to his back and our legs together like lovers might lie. In the morning, he took off his thick army pullover and his rough shirt to wash in the water from a horse-trough outside the door of the barn and it seemed to me that he had a red

mark like some sort of birth defect or wound on his back. I said, 'So, the German race isn't so perfect after all', and he saw the funny side and laughed. I am sure that he never told me his name: I think that he was afraid to do so, in case it led to trouble for him later. I would have remembered his name if he had, as I owe him much.

Until the next time,

Yours, Fishel R.

31

How to finish it? This question keeps dogging me and I do not know how to answer it: I ask myself again and again whether Christopher sat in our house for those days he was with us, trying to decide how to end his life, or whether it was a sudden, impetuous decision; a *crime passionel* against the self. All I know for certain is that he, like my twin, will never really leave me: he is inside me, he comes from me; he is part of what I am.

It is late February, the month of my mother's birth and death. Her life went full circle like a necklace of beads: she died on the twenty-third of the month and was born the day after. I am standing on Cambridge station, waiting for my early morning train to King's Cross, anticipating the rush for a seat, the vying with backpackers as they jostle to get through the train doors and the business talk of the commuters as they rustle their broadsheets. The station-master announces in his thick Cambridgeshire burr: 'The train at platform five is the *o*-eight-twenty-*seven* service to Harwich International.' I imagine my mother's train passing through the station on its way to Liverpool Street, steam billowing up in a thick cloud behind it as it shoots past without stopping, its pistons pumping furiously and its wheels turning in a blur as it heads up from the coast with its cargo of lost souls. Her train from the Harwich ferry was crowded with child after child from Düsseldorf or Dortmund, Berlin or Bielefeld, each one clutching a doll or a comfort-blanket and holding on to their last memories of home until their names and their futures changed beyond recognition.

London and work can wait: I run from platform one to where the Harwich train is standing. The guard has blown his whistle and the train doors are about to close as I jump on board. The train is very quiet. Only a few travellers, bound perhaps for the late-morning ferry from Harwich to the Hook of Holland, sit at the far end of the carriage; otherwise I am left alone to watch the flat countryside and the low clouds go by. The train takes almost two hours to reach the port, passing through small towns and villages along the way, and I imagine all the while the thundering ghost of my mother's locomotive passing through our own three-carriage train; two reels of celluloid film running over and against each other, one fast-forwarding and the other rewinding frame by frame, window by window. Time reversing and time racing on: histories eliding and splicing, blurring into one.

I do not get off the train when it reaches the port terminus, but rather wait the half hour in my seat until the driver walks to the other end of the train and starts her back up again for Cambridge and Liverpool Street. The journey itself is enough: I do not need to go down to the quayside or watch as the lumbering ferries embark or disembark. Nothing is as it was anyway.

I have brought with me on the journey a box-file filled with letters written by Isy to Fishel from the end of the war until his death: a one-sided correspondence, as Fishel's letters of reply are of course absent, half a world away.

Fishel gave the letters to me when we met in Haifa, so that I could look after them and pass them on down through my own family.

As the train winds its way through the flatlands of East Anglia, I leaf through the bundle of perhaps two hundred letters, reading sections at random. Amongst them is a dog-eared affidavit sworn by Isy in 1955 in front of a lawyer at the German consulate in Melbourne:

a document that later helped Fishel to get reparation money from the German government. In its dry language, it outlines the whole story of their friendship with dates and names and facts, and yet tells you nothing.

I, Isy Bernstein of Melbourne in the State of Victoria, Commonwealth of Australia, Teacher, make oath and say as follows:

1. I have known Fishel Rotstein now of Haifa in the country of Israel since before the year 1942.

2. From June 1942 until August 1943 the said Fishel Rotstein and I were both inmates at the Camp at Sternberg. We were then moved with other inmates to a Concentration Camp at Auschwitz Buna where we remained until January, 1945. In January, 1945, we were transferred to the Concentration Camp at Buchenwald where we were detained for about a month. In February, 1945, the said Fishel Rotstein and I were moved to a Concentration Camp at Langenstein and remained there until we escaped in April, 1945.

3. During the periods specified in Paragraph 2 hereof the said Fishel Rotstein and I were constantly together and saw one another practically daily.

4. Since our release the said Fishel Rotstein and I have maintained our friendship and have corresponded with one another at regular intervals. I am satisfied that the Fishel Rotstein now resident in Haifa is identical with the person with whom I was interned during the periods specified in Paragraph 2 hereof.

5. My number during the periods spent by me in

Concentration Camps was 143964 and the same is tattoed on my arm.

Isy Bernstein
21st January 1955

The train pulls into Cambridge station just before one o'clock and I walk through the town back towards our house. As on most other days, I stop at a café on the way home to sit for a while and have a coffee. Through the wide double bay of the café's windows, misted from the heater and the exhalation of its guests, I watch the endless stream of people going about their business and wonder what histories lie behind their being here now, in these precise coordinates of place and this infinitesimal synapse of time. *It's time to start living in the present again*, I say to myself over and over, trying to make myself believe it.

When I get back home, Caroline is in the garden kneeling on the grass and weeding one of the flowerbeds. She looks *radiant*, that is the only word for it: her cheeks are flushed from the cold air and her blonde hair is tied back in a ponytail, exposing her delicate neck and the beautiful curve of her jaw. Something in this moment holds the clarity of recognition that only comes to you once or twice in a lifetime, if you are lucky. I know that she is pregnant and I know for sure that she is what I need. One day we will both be swallowed up by history's endless falling away: the canvas will be blank again, the page unwritten. For now, though, we are here and we are alive.

The green shoots of crocuses and hyacinths are already pushing up through the winter soil.

POSTSCRIPT I

Evidence – material, spoken or written – is how one constructs the story of a life; how one pieces history together. There were elusive bodies of evidence when I was growing up. Material: the heavy, prewar cutlery with which my family ate, whose handles were decorated with a monogram that did not match our English surname. Spoken: those odd turns of phrase coming through my mother's private-school-educated English – dated German exclamations such as '*Donnerwetter!*' ('My goodness!') and curious-sounding words beginning with an un-English '*sch* ', such as '*Schlemiel* ' ('bumbling fool'), '*schickse*' ('non-Jewish girl') and '*Schnitzel* '. Hers was a multicultural Germanic 'otherness': High German, *plattdeutsch*, Austrian and Yiddish language always seemed to seep through the porous boundaries of her adopted English tongue. She could never get over some words: she always referred to her mother as '*Mutti*' – the child's 'mummy' – right into her sixties, when she died. Written: after her death, another crucial piece of evidence emerged. My father, sorting through her possessions, came across a cloth-bound diary and I knew immediately that this was the journal that she had occasionally mentioned as I got older. She had never shown it to me nor, as far as I know, had she ever read it. She always said that it was the diary that 'Uncle Isy wrote in Auschwitz', but she was wrong: he wrote it in a small labour camp in East Brandenburg called Sternberg. Perhaps, in her mind, Auschwitz had become the one word governing the terrible reality of 'the camps'. My father, knowing my fascination with my past, gave me the diary and I suddenly knew what my years of studying the German language had been for. I spent weeks and months deciphering my great-uncle Isy's handwriting, reading the whole of the diary's more than three-hundred-and-sixty pages and translating long passages of it into English. Isy's words form the backbone of this book and I am indebted to him, beyond words.

My mother always spoke in vague generalities about her past and I, self-appointed scrutiniser of our family history and keeper of the collective memory as a child, wanted concrete, specific particulars. What was her father's name? What happened to him? What was her mother's name? What happened to her? Who did my mother live with when she came to England? I fired off staccato questions like a round of machine-gun fire, and they hurt her. Her answers were not always clear: 'He went to America before I was born; I never met him.' 'Her name was Mary. I got a letter one day during the War from the Red Cross, saying that she had been killed in the camps.' 'I lived with an assimilated English-Jewish family in Somerset.'

I always got the impression that she could not understand my curiosity about her past that so obviously upset her. When I started a degree in German and later spent a year at university in Heidelberg when I was twenty-one, a year that saw my mother's death from cancer, her only advice to me was: 'Don't get a German girlfriend.' But I was always drawn to the German language, to its rugged, rasping beauty; I always loved it more than the obvious charms of French at school: a strange atavism; a peculiar perversion of taste; a deliberate contrariness, perhaps. My mother did not teach my brothers and me German at home, although she remained fluent in the language until the end.

The diary's story is one of survival: the surfacing of evidence; the living-through of tragedy; the legacy of individuals who, by extraordinary personal sacrifices, allowed their family names to continue down through the generations. What miracle allowed this diary to survive the upheavals of war, the mass movement of millions of individuals through the camp system, the confiscations, the book-burnings, the air raids and the bombardments? I can now never know its secret history for sure: nearly all of those involved with its story are dead. Only Fishel Rotstein, whom Isy introduces at the very end of his diary, is still alive and living in Haifa. The diary sits on my bookshelf and it compelled me to write this novel, a book woven out of the threads of real and imaginary stories and histories.

'*Ibergekumene tsores iz gut tsu dertseyln*': 'It's good to tell about past troubles.' This is the only Yiddish phrase that I know and I did not learn it from my mother: I learned it from a book.

R.A., London 2006

COMING TO GERMAN
POSTSCRIPT II

I recently learned a fascinating fact: when German forces occupied northern France in the summer of 1940, they switched occupied France to GMT+2, German summer time, while the *zone libre*, Vichy France, stayed on GMT+1. The Germans thus translated French time into German time. Translation is always appropriation.

More than twenty-five years ago now, I began translating passages from my great-uncle Isy Aronowitz's Holocaust diary to use these translated texts – appropriate them – as real-life elements woven into my strongly autobiographical yet fictional debut novel, *Five Amber Beads*. I was not certain when I began the process of translation how appropriate it was to use Isy's diary, witness as it is to so much hardship and suffering, in this way, to borrow his words for my own ends.

But I was fearful that, if I did not do something with Isy's diary, no one might ever read it or even see short excerpts from it. Although I only discovered its full scope and impact by reading it right through from first page to last after I had already made the decision to use it in my novel – the decision to co-author, as it were, the book with my great-uncle – I knew *a priori* that Holocaust diaries are rare survivors and invaluable records of the multiplicity of fates of Jews in Nazi Europe.

The memories, the actualities, were not mine. They were those of a Jew born in Wuppertal-Elberfeld in 1913 who had been deported to the border of Poland, the region of his parents' births in Łódz in the last quarter of the nineteenth century when it was still under Russian authority, in the autumn of 1938 at the age of twenty-five.

My mother's family was small, even though her own mother had four siblings. My mother, born in 1931, was an only child and the only child born into her mother Miriam Aronowitz's immediate family until the 1940s. She never knew her father. If my mother's family had been larger, there would undoubtedly have been more victims. As it was, my mother lost her mother in the Minsk Ghetto and her aunt Hedwig in Auschwitz. There were other Aronowitz aunts, uncles and cousins who had stayed in Łódz and not migrated to Wuppertal-Elberfeld in 1910 with my mother's family, and no doubt some of them died in the Holocaust. There are no records, or at least none that I have been able to trace, of their names and fate. These were erased lives even before they were definitively erased.

Isy Aronowitz was an unusual man, and in an unusual position. Born in Germany when all of his older siblings (including my grandmother) had been born in Łódz in quite another world, he was sent to the Lutheran school near the family home. This, despite him writing to my mother in a letter in 1989:

> *My father came from a very religious family, which are no rarities in those times in Poland or Russia. He knew, so it appeared to me, the entire Torah by heart. Whatever part you would ask him, he could recite it with ease.*

Although he did not have to attend lessons in religion, no doubt the atmosphere, the ambience, of the school rubbed off on him and as a young man in the late 1920s or early 1930s he became a committed adherent of the Austrian philosopher Rudolf Steiner's anthroposophical teachings, which combine an element of low-church Protestantism with more mystical, universally spiritual, esoteric doctrines. His admiration of Steiner's teachings even led Isy to move to Dornach near Basel in Switzerland for a while in the 1930s, where the Goetheanum – the 'epicentre' of anthroposophy – is situated. All this is to say: Isy was a Jew with Christian beliefs, not that this stopped him from being deported by the Nazis to the Polish border in 1938 as a non-German, or spending years in the Łódz Ghetto; in the small labour camp of Sternberg in Brandenburg; in Auschwitz; and, finally, in Buchenwald and its pendant camp, Langenstein.

Identity, like history, is not black and white. We might define ourselves one way, while others (in Isy's case, the Nazis) define us in quite another. In one sense, the Nazis were right: Isy was a Jew, born of a Jewish mother – Perla Fajga Wermund, my great-grandmother – and in another sense they missed the point completely. Isy saw himself as a Christian and, unlike other close members of his family, despite the best efforts of mid-twentieth-century history, he did not worship in the synagogue.

Translating parts of Isy's diary was a journey into the barely known. Not only did I know very little about the Łódz Ghetto, I also knew nothing about the Sternberg labour camp where much of the diary is set. I think that no one did. It is barely mentioned in the literature on the Nazi camp system. As far as I can establish, Isy's account of this small labour camp, inhabited mostly by Jewish inmates, is the only one known.

Translating the diary was, then, a privilege and an historically important project. It records with bruising honesty how he as *Unterführer* – the representative of the inmates to the *Kommandant* – had to draft the camp's rules and enforce the death penalty handed down by the *Kommandant*, these plain-spoken horrors counterpointed with his recollections of Christmases past and his thoughts on nature, events in the theatre of war, anthroposophy-flavoured comment and acute observations of his fellow inmates. I kept on having to remind myself that Isy was under thirty when he wrote the diary.

Translating the diary was a revelation in another sense: I began to realise what my years of learning German at school and university had been about. Although my mother remained fluent in German until the end of her life – it was, after all, her mother tongue – us boys had never been taught a word of German at home. My three older brothers do not know the language. Reading Isy's diary I realised that I, the self-appointed family archivist and researcher, had equipped myself with the key to unlocking my family's past: the language in which they conducted their lives after 1910.

Both striving to learn to speak and read German and pushing to uncover hidden traces of my mother's family history have always felt like a kind of going against the grain, things for which I have worked long and hard but that have not always been met with immediate understanding by my family and friends. It is as if I have retreated backwards in time and place to a Polish-German-Jewish life to which I have no connection: I am, after all, English and did not grow up Jewish. My childhood in the 1970s was one of Cotswold-stone cottages, wellies, hills, woods and streams: an unbridgeable remove from my mother's early life and the life of her forebears.

So where does my need to retrace those steps come from? I think that it all started with a strong sense of injustice. Even as quite a young child I knew that my mother had lost her mother, and why. I knew that my mother had come to England alone aged eight. I knew that my mother had suffered terribly as a child; that she had been completely uprooted from her life and had lost the person who meant most to her in the world, and I somehow needed to try to renegotiate these things, to understand them.

My early life was as different from Isy's childhood and young adulthood in Wuppertal as his life was from his parents' lives in Łódz. These shifts, these migrations, of the Aronowitz family from White Russia to Wuppertal to the west of England had seen its surname almost lost, its religion also, and that lack of context was the very thing that compelled me to find some.

Born Richard Mercer, I write under the name Richard Aronowitz to keep this family surname alive. Of the surviving Aronowitz family – Isy's older brother Abraham fled to Holland with his wife Chana in the second half of the 1930s and then on to Melbourne – none has the name, as Abraham and Chana changed their surname to Arnow when they arrived in Australia. They had two daughters, my mother's cousins, and no sons and their daughters lost even their new surname when they married.

The Aronowitz family name is not then, in the usual course of things, my own; German is not my mother tongue; I was born in 1970, twenty-five years after the end of the war and the liberation of the camps; I never knew my grandmother and only met Isy twice, when I was a young boy and knew next-to-nothing about him and what he and his siblings had been through. In my view, all of this makes me more, not less, qualified to act as the translator of Isy's words and as a conduit for my family history. I can look on it all with a certain objectivity, if not exactly distance.

And yet, and yet: it felt like a kind of trespassing. Diaries are written for the writer, not the reader; they are almost never written for publication. It was nigh-on impossible to decide which parts of Isy's diary to include in *Five Amber Beads*, which parts to publish, and which parts – by far the greater majority – to leave unseen by anyone but me. My choices were ultimately ones of cadence and rhythm: which parts fitted best into the structure and flow of my novel, slotted in as they were as chapters in their own right, a second narrative voice, between my fictional text? Which best captured Isy's predicament, his extraordinary character, his knife-edge moral and emotional dilemmas? This act of editing, of weighing up, made me uncomfortable. I just hope that I did the diary justice, for who knows if it will ever see the light of day between other covers.

I was perhaps most affected not by the horrors of Isy's daily life, described by him in his vivid and unusually insightful prose, but by his copying out in the diary of postcards and letters that he receives in Sternberg from his sisters Miriam and Hedwig, my grandmother and great-aunt. More than eighty years since their deaths, these are the only words that I have directly from them. This is Isy's diary entry for the 16th October 1941:

Yesterday, after a long silence, I received a letter from my sister Hedwig in Warsaw. Its contents amazed me, describing the reality of the situation there. She writes the following words: "The people here fight with such a bitter despair over their daily bread that you often ask yourself where they find this last strength. From early morning until late at night, and often during the night itself, you hear their shouts and their cries, "I am hungry: bread, destitution, death." In every street you see these poor people lying there crying; many swollen, many emaciated like skeletons. Only skin and bone – all from hunger. There are thousands of them... Just as terrible as the hunger is this epidemic. The disease is called typhus and it persecutes people wherever they go. In every house there is at least one person with the fever and those that get it rarely recover. Often, when I see the high walls that cut us off from the so-called better people, a great yearning for freedom grips me. The world is so beautiful and so wide. Life could be wonderful if it were not for man and his hatred."

It is not just that Isy and his sisters are going through threefold hell, it is that these members of the family were lost, and yet here are their voices, long dormant in the unread diary and suddenly alive for us to hear again.

How many voices from the Warsaw Ghetto have survived in writing for posterity as Hedwig's has here? I do not know for sure, but I do know that making it possible for her voice, and of course the voices of Miriam and Isy, to reach an audience – by no means a huge one, as *Five Amber Beads* was no international bestseller – was one of the central ambitions of the whole endeavour, alongside my personal hopes of fulfilment as a creative writer.

Growing up in England as the son of a mother who was a Jewish refugee from Nazi Germany and having been brought up essentially without a word of German at home, other than my mother's occasional slips back into her mother tongue, I think that the chances of my becoming near-fluent in German and using it as a tool for translating Isy's diary might have been viewed as very slight when I was a child. So how did I come to German? It all goes back to Isy: it was he who went back into Germany from Switzerland to try to get my mother and her mother out of Germany; it was he who managed, at least, to help get my mother out; and it was he who, with his unbreakable belief in anthroposophy and the teachings of Rudolf Steiner, arranged for her to go to a Steiner school in England after she had arrived on the *Kindertransport*.

Rudolf Steiner schools in Britain are fee-paying private schools, yet during the war they took in Jewish refugee children for free. Years later, when her children had reached school age, my mother wanted to pay back the Steiner system by sending all of her four boys to its schools. These schools place great emphasis on the arts and on the teaching of foreign languages. The seeds for my coming to German were, then, sown by Isy himself: they just needed the right conditions to germinate and grow. I had a sensitive enough ear and a logical enough mind to find the learning of foreign languages quite straightforward and, without knowing it, I had equipped myself by the end of university with exactly the right tools to begin work on what has been in many ways the most important project of my life: trying to recover the erased lives of my mother's family.

Translating elements of Isy's diary has been a fundamentally important part of this endeavour, letting me hear not only his voice, ringing out like a bell from the silence of history, but also the voices of other members of my family who I never had the good fortune to meet.

Richard Aronowitz, Oxford, 2025

GLOSSARY

Gemeinde – community
Gefreiter – Private
Judenrat – Jewish council
Kindertransport – children's transport
Shtetl – small Jewish town or village
Tagebuch – diary
Unterführer – deputy leader
Wehrbezirkskommando – military district command
Wehrkreis – military district
Wehrmacht – German army during the Third Reich
Wehrpass – army identity card

AMSTERDAM PUBLISHERS HOLOCAUST LIBRARY

The series **Holocaust Survivor Memoirs World War II** consists of the following autobiographies of survivors:

Outcry. Holocaust Memoirs, by Manny Steinberg

Hank Brodt Holocaust Memoirs. A Candle and a Promise, by Deborah Donnelly

The Dead Years. Holocaust Memoirs, by Joseph Schupack

Rescued from the Ashes. The Diary of Leokadia Schmidt, Survivor of the Warsaw Ghetto, by Leokadia Schmidt

My Lvov. Holocaust Memoir of a twelve-year-old Girl, by Janina Hescheles

Remembering Ravensbrück. From Holocaust to Healing, by Natalie Hess

Wolf. A Story of Hate, by Zeev Scheinwald with Ella Scheinwald

Save my Children. An Astonishing Tale of Survival and its Unlikely Hero, by Leon Kleiner with Edwin Stepp

Holocaust Memoirs of a Bergen-Belsen Survivor & Classmate of Anne Frank, by Nanette Blitz Konig

Defiant German - Defiant Jew. A Holocaust Memoir from inside the Third Reich, by Walter Leopold with Les Leopold

In a Land of Forest and Darkness. The Holocaust Story of two Jewish Partisans, by Sara Lustigman Omelinski

Holocaust Memories. Annihilation and Survival in Slovakia, by Paul Davidovits

From Auschwitz with Love. The Inspiring Memoir of Two Sisters' Survival, Devotion and Triumph Told by Manci Grunberger Beran & Ruth Grunberger Mermelstein, by Daniel Seymour

Remetz. Resistance Fighter and Survivor of the Warsaw Ghetto, by Jan Yohay Remetz

My March Through Hell. A Young Girl's Terrifying Journey to Survival, by Halina Kleiner with Edwin Stepp

Roman's Journey, by Roman Halter

Beyond Borders. Escaping the Holocaust and Fighting the Nazis. 1938-1948, by Rudi Haymann

The Engineers. A memoir of survival through World War II in Poland and Hungary, by Henry Reiss

Spark of Hope. An Autobiography, by Luba Wrobel Goldberg

Footnote to History. From Hungary to America. The Memoir of a Holocaust Survivor, by Andrew Laszlo

Farewell Atlantis. Recollections, by Valentīna Freimane

The Courtyard. A memoir, by Ben Parket and Alexa Morris

Run, Mendel Run, by Milton H. Schwartz

The series **Holocaust Survivor True Stories** consists of the following biographies:

Among the Reeds. The true story of how a family survived the Holocaust, by Tammy Bottner

A Holocaust Memoir of Love & Resilience. Mama's Survival from Lithuania to America, by Ettie Zilber

Living among the Dead. My Grandmother's Holocaust Survival Story of Love and Strength, by Adena Bernstein Astrowsky

Heart Songs. A Holocaust Memoir, by Barbara Gilford

Shoes of the Shoah. The Tomorrow of Yesterday, by Dorothy Pierce

Hidden in Berlin. A Holocaust Memoir, by Evelyn Joseph Grossman

Separated Together. The Incredible True WWII Story of Soulmates Stranded an Ocean Apart, by Kenneth P. Price, Ph.D.

The Man Across the River. The incredible story of one man's will to survive the Holocaust, by Zvi Wiesenfeld

If Anyone Calls, Tell Them I Died. A Memoir, by Emanuel (Manu) Rosen

The House on Thrömerstrasse. A Story of Rebirth and Renewal in the Wake of the Holocaust, by Ron Vincent

Dancing with my Father. His hidden past. Her quest for truth. How Nazi Vienna shaped a family's identity, by Jo Sorochinsky

The Story Keeper. Weaving the Threads of Time and Memory - A Memoir, by Fred Feldman

Krisia's Silence. The Girl who was not on Schindler's List, by Ronny Hein

Defying Death on the Danube. A Holocaust Survival Story, by Debbie J. Callahan with Henry Stern

A Doorway to Heroism. A decorated German-Jewish Soldier who became an American Hero, by W. Jack Romberg

The Shoemaker's Son. The Life of a Holocaust Resister, by Laura Beth Bakst

The Redhead of Auschwitz. A True Story, by Nechama Birnbaum

Land of Many Bridges. My Father's Story, by Bela Ruth Samuel Tenenholtz

Creating Beauty from the Abyss. The Amazing Story of Sam Herciger, Auschwitz Survivor and Artist, by Lesley Ann Richardson

On Sunny Days We Sang. A Holocaust Story of Survival and Resilience, by Jeannette Grunhaus de Gelman

Painful Joy. A Holocaust Family Memoir, by Max J. Friedman

I Give You My Heart. A True Story of Courage and Survival, by Wendy Holden

In the Time of Madmen, by Mark A. Prelas

Monsters and Miracles. Horror, Heroes and the Holocaust, by Ira Wesley Kitmacher

Flower of Vlora. Growing up Jewish in Communist Albania, by Anna Kohen

Aftermath: Coming of Age on Three Continents. A Memoir, by Annette Libeskind Berkovits

Not a real Enemy. The True Story of a Hungarian Jewish Man's Fight for Freedom, by Robert Wolf

Zaidy's War. Four Armies, Three Continents, Two Brothers. One Man's Impossible Story of Endurance, by Martin Bodek

The Glassmaker's Son. Looking for the World my Father left behind in Nazi Germany, by Peter Kupfer

The Apprentice of Buchenwald. The True Story of the Teenage Boy Who Sabotaged Hitler's War Machine, by Oren Schneider

Good for a Single Journey, by Helen Joyce

Burying the Ghosts. She escaped Nazi Germany only to have her life torn apart by the woman she saved from the camps: her mother, by Sonia Case

American Wolf. From Nazi Refugee to American Spy. A True Story, by Audrey Birnbaum

Bipolar Refugee. A Saga of Survival and Resilience, by Peter Wiesner

In the Wake of Madness. My Family's Escape from the Nazis, by Bettie Lennett Denny

Before the Beginning and After the End, by Hymie Anisman

I Will Give Them an Everlasting Name. Jacksonville's Stories of the Holocaust, by Samuel Cox

Hiding in Holland. A Resistance Memoir, by Shulamit Reinharz

The Ghosts on the Wall. A Grandson's Memoir of the Holocaust, by Kenneth D. Wald

Thirteen in Auschwitz. My grandmother's fight to stay human, by Lauren Meyerowitz Port

The series **Jewish Children in the Holocaust** consists of the following autobiographies of Jewish children hidden during WWII in the Netherlands:

Searching for Home. The Impact of WWII on a Hidden Child,
by Joseph Gosler

Sounds from Silence. Reflections of a Child Holocaust Survivor, Psychiatrist and Teacher, by Robert Krell

Sabine's Odyssey. A Hidden Child and her Dutch Rescuers,
by Agnes Schipper

The Journey of a Hidden Child, by Harry Pila and Robin Black

The series **New Jewish Fiction** consists of the following novels, written by Jewish authors. All novels are set in the time during or after the Holocaust.

The Corset Maker. A Novel, by Annette Libeskind Berkovits

Escaping the Whale. The Holocaust is over. But is it ever over for the next generation? by Ruth Rotkowitz

When the Music Stopped. Willy Rosen's Holocaust, by Casey Hayes

Hands of Gold. One Man's Quest to Find the Silver Lining in Misfortune, by Roni Robbins

The Girl Who Counted Numbers. A Novel, by Roslyn Bernstein

There was a garden in Nuremberg. A Novel, by Navina Michal Clemerson

The Butterfly and the Axe, by Omer Bartov

To Live Another Day. A Novel, by Elizabeth Rosenberg

The Right to Happiness. After all they went through. Stories, by Helen Schary Motro

Five Amber Beads, by Richard Aronowitz

To Love Another Day. A Novel, by Elizabeth Rosenberg

Cursing the Darkness. A Novel about Loss and Recovery, by Joanna Rosenthall

The series **Holocaust Heritage** consists of the following memoirs by 2G:

The Cello Still Sings. A Generational Story of the Holocaust and of the Transformative Power of Music, by Janet Horvath

The Fire and the Bonfire. A Journey into Memory, by Ardyn Halter

The Silk Factory: Finding Threads of My Family's True Holocaust Story, by Michael Hickins

Winter Light. The Memoir of a Child of Holocaust Survivors, by Grace Feuerverger

Out from the Shadows. Growing up with Holocaust Survivor Parents, by Willie Handler

Hidden in Plain Sight. A Family Memoir and the Untold Story of the Holocaust in Serbia, by Julie Brill

The Unspeakable. Breaking my family's silence surrounding the Holocaust, by Nicola Hanefeld

Eighteen for Life. Surviving the Holocaust, by Helen Schamroth

Austrian Again. Reclaiming a Lost Legacy, by Anne Hand

The series **Holocaust Books for Young Adults** consists of the following novels, based on true stories:

The Boy behind the Door. How Salomon Kool Escaped the Nazis. Inspired by a True Story, by David Tabatsky

Running for Shelter. A True Story, by Suzette Sheft

The Precious Few. An Inspirational Saga of Courage based on True Stories, by David Twain with Art Twain

Dark Shadows Hover, by Jordan Steven Sher

The Sun will Shine Again, by Cynthia Goldstein Monsour

The series **WWII Historical Fiction** consists of the following novels, some of which are based on true stories:

Mendelevski's Box. A Heartwarming and Heartbreaking Jewish Survivor's Story, by Roger Swindells

A Quiet Genocide. The Untold Holocaust of Disabled Children in WWII Germany, by Glenn Bryant

The Knife-Edge Path, by Patrick T. Leahy

Brave Face. The Inspiring WWII Memoir of a Dutch/German Child, by I. Caroline Crocker and Meta A. Evenbly

When We Had Wings. The Gripping Story of an Orphan in Janusz Korczak's Orphanage. A Historical Novel, by Tami Shem-Tov

Jacob's Courage. Romance and Survival amidst the Horrors of War, by Charles S. Weinblatt

A Semblance of Justice. Based on true Holocaust experiences, by Wolf Holles

Under the Pink Triangle. Where forbidden love meets unspeakable evil, by Katie Moore

Amsterdam Publishers Newsletter

Subscribe to our Newsletter by selecting the menu at the top (right) of amsterdampublishers.com or scan the QR-code below.

www.ingramcontent.com/pod-product-compliance
Lightning Source LLC
LaVergne TN
LVHW091547070526
838199LV00024B/570/J